Pocket Guide
to the
Bahamas

FODOR'S TRAVEL PUBLICATIONS

are compiled, researched, and edited by an international team of travel writers, field correspondents, and editors. The series, which now almost covers the globe, was founded by Eugene Fodor in 1936.

OFFICES
New York & London

Fodor's Pocket Guide to the Bahamas

Editor: Vernon Nahrgang
Area Editor: Anita Gates
Cartographer: David Lindroth
Drawings: Michael Kaplan
Cover Photograph: Paul Barton

Cover Design: Vignelli Associates

Fodor's 89
Pocket Guide
to the
Bahamas

Anita Gates

This book contains material previously published as
Fodor's Fun in the Bahamas

FODOR'S TRAVEL PUBLICATIONS, INC.
New York & London

ISBN 0–679–01626–0

MANUFACTURED IN THE UNITED STATES OF AMERICA
10 9 8 7 6 5 4 3 2 1

CONTENTS

CONTENTS

Maps and Plans

FOREWORD

Geography and convenient airline and cruise schedules make the Bahamas an ideal foreign destination for U.S. and Canadian travelers in search of the brief getaway vacation. *Fodor's Pocket Guide to the Bahamas* is intended for just those short-term visitors who want a concise account of what they will find at the best hotels and restaurants and the shopping and recreation opportunities that await them in the islands.

Travelers who plan to spend more time in the Bahamas, or seek additional information on history, customs, and unusual travel options, as well as those who would simply like to have a second opinion, will want to consult *Fodor's Bahamas* for in-depth coverage of the archipelago.

While every care has been taken to assure the accuracy of the information in this guide, the passage of time will always bring change, and consequently the publisher cannot accept responsibility for errors that may occur.

All prices and opening times quoted here are based on information available to us at press time. Hours and admission fees may change, however, and the prudent traveler will avoid inconvenience by calling ahead.

Fodor's wants to hear about your travel experiences, both pleasant and unpleasant. When a hotel or restaurant fails to live up to its billing, let us know and we will investigate the complaint and revise our entries where the facts warrant it.

Send your letters to the editors of Fodor's Travel Publications, 201 E. 50th Street, New York, NY 10022, or 30–32 Bedford Square, London WC1B 3SG, England.

INTRODUCTION TO
THE BAHAMAS

The Bahamas have always moved to the rhythm of the times, as though this island chain could alter its essential character with the changes in public taste, with the constantly evolving image of what travel ought to be.

In the 1860s, when it first seemed a good idea to attract visitors simply with the appeal of travel as novelty, its ports were exotic and faraway by the standards of the day.

In the 1920s, when Americans reveled in their country's newfound wealth and in the joys of travel as a form of play, the luxurious yachts of the Astors and the Vanderbilts sailed into the harbors of Nassau. What better place to sit out the Jazz Age than here, surrounded by the clearest, calmest blue waters in the New World?

1

In the 1940s, when an old world of grace and charm seemed to be slipping away, a change hastened by the winds of world war, the Duke and Duchess of Windsor came—he as the islands' appointed governor—and made the Bahamas a royal refuge. In the halls of Graycliff in old Nassau, the manners and civility of a fading European aristocracy were alive and well and appeared to be perfectly at home.

And now, when the frequent flyer is the envied world traveler of the age, the Bahamas have emerged again as ideal destinations. The grand tour is an anachronism. North Americans, immersed in their fast-lane schedules and given more vacation time than any past generation, have created the long weekend and claimed it as their right. Gone is the tradition of a solid year of hard work followed by a single two-week or three-week holiday. The fashionable late-20th-century traveler takes much shorter vacations but lots of them.

The Bahamas fit the bill beautifully. Their proximity makes getaways easy, particularly for U.S. residents in the South and East. The northernmost islands are due east of Palm Beach, Florida, with the western tip of Grand Bahama only 75 miles away. Bimini, further south, is equally close to Miami. And although the Bahamas stretch 760 miles southeast across the Tropic of Cancer, the southernmost island (Great Inagua) is just off the coast of Cuba, about 100 miles north of Haiti.

For Americans, Canadians, and the English, the Bahamas present a comfortable combination of the foreign and the familiar. Most of all, they are wonderfully varied. Of the 700 or so islands and cays in the Bahamas chain, only about two dozen are inhabited, and they are as different as sister islands can be.

In the "big cities" of Nassau and Freeport visitors find busy shops, formal restaurants, casinos, and full-scale resorts with grand sweeping lobbies and nightly stage shows. On the secluded islands, vacationers can spend entire weeks barefoot at the tiniest of beachfront hotels and guest houses. And many places fall between the two extremes.

Nassau, the Bahamas' capital city, set on New Providence Island, is the first part of the Bahamas most visitors see. Whether you stay at one of the large modern resorts on Cable Beach, in a smaller hotel in old Nassau (nearer the downtown area), or across the bridge on Paradise Island, you can choose to be as busy or as lazy as you please.

White-sand beaches, ocean swimming, pools, snorkeling, scuba diving, sailing, windsurfing, and parasailing await the visitor. There are tennis courts, golf courses, health clubs, and organized activities for every day of the week. When it's cloudy, you can spend the day downtown on Bay Street looking for perfumes, watches, emeralds, leather goods, straw bags, resort wear, or gifts. And at almost any hour you can get a cupful of quarters and settle in at the nearest casino.

On Grand Bahama you're most likely to stay in Freeport/Lucaya. Freeport is a gambler's and shopper's paradise, with its huge Moorish casino and an international shopping center where visitors can spend their winnings on jewelry, clothing, glassware, art, and fashions from around the world. A longtime favorite of divers, Lucaya is the more casual side of town, with its hotels right on the beach.

After New Providence and Grand Bahama islands, everywhere else in the Bahamas is known collectively as the Family Islands. But that name may be misleading; they were formerly called the Out Islands, a designation that conveys better their situation: remote, cut off from urban life, underdeveloped.

Perhaps the best known of the Family Islands is Eleuthera, with each of its towns a destination unto itself. Harbour Island attracts a combination of old money and young boaters and divers to its small pink-sand resorts. In Governor's Harbour the Club Med is devoted primarily to scuba diving. Further south, there are elegant resorts and homes in Windermere, Winding Rock, and Rock Sound.

The Abacos, a boater's paradise, offer a particularly friendly island welcome. Marsh Harbour, the liveliest town and the most casual, is filled with boaters, other U.S. vacationers, and nightlife. The most formal part of Great Abaco is Treasure Cay, as is the resort of the same name. Green Turtle Cay falls somewhere in between, with resorts that draw yachtsmen, honeymooners, and the world-weary of all categories. To reach the most secluded Abaco hotels of all, take a ferry to Hopetown.

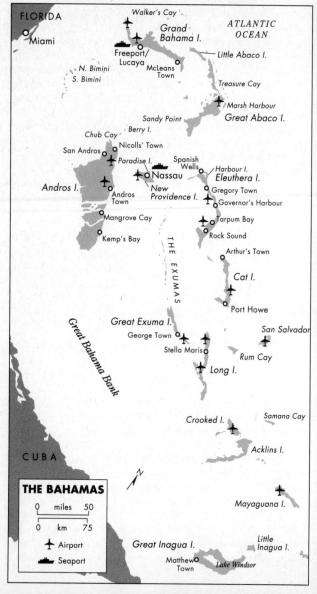

FLORIDA

ATLANTIC OCEAN

Miami

Walker's Cay

Grand Bahama I.

Freeport/ Lucaya

Little Abaco I.

McLeans Town

N. Bimini
S. Bimini

Treasure Cay

Marsh Harbour

Great Abaco I.

Sandy Point

Berry I.

Chub Cay

Nicolls' Town

San Andros

Paradise I.

Spanish Wells

Harbour I.

Eleuthera I.

Nassau

Andros I.

New Providence I.

Andros Town

Gregory Town

Governor's Harbour

Mangrove Cay

Tarpum Bay

Rock Sound

Kemp's Bay

THE EXUMAS

Arthur's Town

Cat I.

Port Howe

Great Exuma I.

George Town

San Salvador

Great Bahama Bank

Stella Maris

Rum Cay

Long I.

Crooked I.

Samana Cay

Acklins I.

CUBA

N

THE BAHAMAS

| 0 | miles | 50 |
| 0 | km | 75 |

✈ Airport
⛴ Seaport

Mayaguana I.

Great Inagua I.

Little Inagua I.

Matthew Town

Lake Windsor

Andros is the largest of the islands yet one of the least developed. Its best-known resort, Small Hope Bay Lodge, a mecca for divers, lies just off the world's third largest barrier reef.

Exuma may be the world's best yachting destination, not only during its annual Regatta but year-round, for North Americans and other visitors who love the challenge of its cays. Bonefishing is an important sport here. George Town, the center of activity, has an almost rowdy nightlife of locals and visiting boaters. Some of the Bahamas most beautiful (and lesser known) beaches are here, too, particularly on Little Exuma and on Stocking Island.

Bimini is Hemingway country, the big-game fishing capital of the world; it exists almost exclusively for these purposes. Its name found its way into headlines again in 1987 when Gary Hart, Donna Rice, and friends vacationed here on a boat named *Monkey Business*. The mood in Bimini is American, with rock music nearly always in the background and the names of Florida sportsmen dominating the guest registers.

What of the other 700 or so Bahamian islands? They've been called the "Far Out Islands"; some of them have only one resort or a few tiny guest houses, others are true desert islands even today. Yet each seems to have its own special appeal, and many of them can be wonderful places for the vacationer who defines travel as total escape.

The Bahamas' modern history began on October 12, 1492, when Christopher Columbus discovered the New World. Historians still argue about exactly which island he landed on that day: Was it the one now called San Salvador, or was it Samana Cay, some 65 miles to the southeast?

Historians do agree that the people who already lived there called their island Guanahani. They were Arawak Indians, the Lucayans, believed to have been in the area for at least 700 years, having fled the less friendly Carib Indians in the islands to the south (the Lesser Antilles in what we now call the Caribbean).

The Lucayans taught the Spaniards to make hammocks, and the Spaniards repaid them by taking them prisoner and shipping them off to work on other islands of New Spain.

Columbus went on to island-hop, visiting the spots now known as Rum Cay, Long Island, Crooked Island, and the Ragged Islands. He called the area *Baja Mar,* Spanish for shallow sea, thereby naming the entire island chain.

Ponce de Leon was sent to Bimini in the early 1500s to look for the fountain of youth. Otherwise, European explorers seemed uninterested in the Bahamas.

In 1629 England formally claimed the Bahamas, and in the 1640s the first island was settled. That island was called Cigatoo, but the English and Bermudan settlers, fleeing religious disputes back home, changed its name to Eleuthera, the Greek word for freedom.

New Providence Island was settled in the 1650s. When the tobacco, cotton, and sugar cane crops turned out to be less profitable than hoped, the corrupt governors of the era figured they could make ends meet by allowing the capital, Charles Towne (renamed Nassau later in the century), and the surrounding waters to become a refuge for the English, Dutch, and French pirates who preyed on Spanish ships.

In 1717 King George I appointed Captain Woodes Rogers the Bahamas' first royal governor and sent him in to clean up the mess. He did such a good job that *Expulsis Piratis, Restituta Commercia* (pirates expelled, commerce restored) remained the islands' motto for more than 250 years.

The American Revolution brought another wave of settlement to the Bahamas. Loyalists—those who had opposed American independence from England—left their homes in New York and New England or their plantations in Virginia and the Carolinas to start a new life in these British islands. Between 1784 and 1789 the population of the Bahamas tripled. Seven out of ten Bahamians were slaves, brought by the Americans, until the United Kingdom Emancipation Act of 1834 gave them their freedom.

By the time of the American Civil War, the farsighted in the Bahamas had already passed the first Tourism Encouragement Act, arranged steamship service between New York and Nassau, and built the Royal Victoria Hotel. Invalids had long been coming to the Bahamas, seeking a rest cure beneath its warm, sunny skies.

Once the war between the states began, blockade-running proved bigger business than tourism. In the 1920s, during America's Prohibition era, rum-running and bootlegging were equally profitable.

By the time Prohibition was repealed in 1933, the Bahamas had entered a new era: The age of tourism had begun. Yachts dotted Nassau's harbor, new beach hotels were built, and in 1929 a small airline called Pan American inaugurated daily flights between Miami and Nassau.

In 1973 the Bahamas achieved political independence. By choice, the new island nation remained in the Commonwealth of Nations with the British monarch as its head of state. A new national motto, "Forward, Upward, Onward Together," replaced the 18th-century commemoration of the pirates' expulsion.

Today the Bahamas are governed by the black majority, and blacks increasingly hold positions of power in tourism and other industries.

By and large, the Bahamians are a religious people. The churches are filled, the signs at souvenir stands may include a "God bless you," and more than one visitor has approached a poolside bar or entered a shop to find employees engaged in a heated philosophical discussion of the Ten Commandments.

As in many countries, people tend to be friendlier in small towns than in big cities—or, in the Bahamas, on the smaller islands rather than on the more heavily populated ones, New Providence, Paradise Island, and Grand Bahama.

The language throughout the Bahamas is English, often spoken with a special Bahamian lilt and with more British influence than American. The English-speaking visitor has only to learn to pronounce cay *(key)* and conch *(conk)* properly in order to fit right in.

You'll find conch on the menu throughout the Bahamas, in a wide variety of forms from chowder to fritters. You'll also find the islands' special rum drinks, the Bahama Mama, Yellowbird, and the infamous Goombay Smash. Still another commonplace is Androsia, the attractive batik resort wear made on the island of Andros; it appears in almost every hotel shop and shopping center, and you'll see it worn by a number of your fellow tourists.

Wherever you go throughout the islands, you're sure to feel the Bahamas' continuing appeal: a place for play, for getaways, for winding down to whatever degree you want. Here is a place just exotic enough to let you forget worry and stress—for a season, a week, or a three-day or four-day weekend in which every long, lazy hour counts.

GENERAL

INFORMATION

With an average winter temperature of 70 degrees and an average summer day at 81 degrees, the Bahamas are a year-round destination. Yet there are definite high and low seasons.

If you are taking a winter vacation, remember that the Bahamas are not technically in the Caribbean. Most of the best-known islands are just east of Florida, and the southernmost destinations are still well north of Haiti and Puerto Rico. Although winter temperatures rarely fall below 60, the unusual does happen. A few resorts may take pride in telling you that they've actually used their big, normally decorative fireplaces during Christmas and January chills.

Summer is the rainy season, and the islands get an average of 46 inches per year. Happily, Bahamian rainstorms are usually gentle and brief. Many seasoned travelers don't even bother to get out of the pool, knowing the storm will be over before they could towel themselves dry.

High season is winter, usually early December through Easter or mid-April, whichever comes later. And although daytime weather may be much the same here in January or July, your fellow visitors are likely to be very different from season to season.

Those who winter in the Bahamas tend to be older, richer, and from more distant places; there are more northeasterners, for instance. Those who come in the summer tend to be younger, more budget-minded and more often from Florida or other parts of the South. "In the winter, most of the traveler's checks we get at the front desk are fifties and hundreds," reports one hotelier. "In the summer, they're tens and twenties." Honeymooners come at all times of year.

To every rule there is an exception, and some islands experience a completely different cycle. At the dive resorts, like Small Hope Bay Lodge on Andros, June is just as busy as February; at Bimini, where the number of visitors is governed by the kind of fish that are biting, summer is by far the busiest time of the year.

Most Bahamian resorts stay open year-round; of those that close temporarily, most take a one-month or two-month break between August and October.

WHAT TO WEAR

Your wardrobe depends on your destination and on how you plan to spend your days and nights.

Nassau is the big city of the Bahamas and demands a little more formality than other locations. Most Nassau and Paradise Island hotels are accustomed to guests walking in or near the lobby in swimsuits, preferably with cover-ups. If there's a separate pool elevator, use it. If not, make it clear that you're just passing through.

A shopping expedition to Nassau's Bay Street or to Freeport's International Bazaar calls for real clothes, not beachwear. Modest shorts, jeans, or cotton pants, worn with any not-too-bare top, is fine shopping wear for men or women. Sundresses with comfortable sandals can be good for this. (Even in the very casual Out Islands, local residents frown on swimsuits on the streets. Worse yet, they sometimes make comments about them as the guests pass.)

There's not a single restaurant in the Bahamas at which you wouldn't feel comfortable dressed very casually for lunch. Dinner is another matter. At the more elegant restaurants, jackets are required for men. Ties are still optional. However, many business travelers come to Nassau and Paradise Island, and they tend to wear ties, so gentlemen may want to go along with the trend. For women, dressing up for an elegant dinner means putting on any nice sundress or pants outfit, but with dressy sandals. Female business travelers and Bahamian women in business probably will wear panty hose, but you don't have to. After all, this *is* a vacation.

The only visitors who get really dressed up are those attending conventions who have their business images in mind. You'll see them at the Cable Beach, the Paradise Towers, and other hotels that cater to these groups.

The Out Islands dress code, by comparison, makes Nassau casual look like opening night at the opera. The rule: Never dress up for anything. Even hotel managers often wear T-shirts and shorts on the job.

On most Out Islands you'll be able to have breakfast and lunch in the sloppiest of resort wear. T-shirts and shorts, swimsuits and cover-ups, bare feet or flip-flops are fine. So is wet hair.

People on the Out Islands do tend to change clothes for dinner. That is, they shower, shampoo, and put on a different set of casual clothes. Men can get away with shorts at many Out Island resorts. So can women, but most prefer to wear sundresses, with either bare feet or flat sandals.

One notable exception to this rule is Treasure Cay in Abaco. Although quite casual during the day, its restaurants call for men in jackets at dinnertime.

One other wardrobe note: If you're going to the Bahamas in winter, pack a light jacket or sweater. Chances are you won't need it, but the evenings do occasionally turn chilly.

WHAT TO PACK

If you have a favorite suntan lotion, pick up an extra tube at home and toss it into your bag. Some popular U.S. brands can be hard to find, particularly outside the Nassau/Paradise Island and Freeport/Lucaya hubs. Locally manufactured sun-care products are more widely available.

If you're planning to stay in a cottage, villa, or any kind of resort in which you'll have to walk back to your room on dark pathways, bring a flashlight. Some resorts light the grounds adequately; others may not. The flashlight could come in handy, too, if you get lost (or change your mind) during a romantic moonlit stroll.

And if you're visiting the Out Islands, take insect repellent. Brands like Cutter's really work, and the comfort can make a big difference as you attempt to relax by the sea.

TIME

The Bahamas are on Eastern Time. When it's noon in the Bahamas, it's 9 A.M. in Los Angeles and Vancouver, 10 A.M. in Phoenix, 11 A.M. in Chicago, noon in New York and Toronto, and 5 P.M. in London, England.

SEASONAL EVENTS

Most of the Bahamas' big annual events require reservations months (or more) in advance. The Family Island Regatta in Exuma, Abaco's fishing tournament (both in April), and Bimini's blue marlin tournament (in June) are examples. The year's most colorful Junkanoo parades are held on Boxing Day (December 26) and New Year's Day throughout the islands, and that, too, means making reservations well in advance.

One of the most successful events has been the Goombay Festival each summer. Designed simply to add a little excitement to the slow off-season, Goombay has grown to include organized events almost every night, particularly in Nassau,

Paradise Island, and Freeport. This can mean an outdoor festival, parade, tea party, jogging contest, or almost anything else that's fun.

Watch out for holidays that the Bahamians celebrate that are unfamiliar to us, especially if you're planning a short trip. Otherwise you might arrive to find shops and many restaurants closed on the one day you'd planned to explore them. Whit Monday (seven weeks after Easter), Emancipation Day (first Monday in August), and Discovery Day (October 12) are among the most important.

GETTING THERE

Airlines. Many visitors coming from North America fly to Nassau. Regularly scheduled commercial flights depart from a number of U.S. and Canadian cities.

Among major airlines that serve the Bahamas are Air Canada, British Airways, Delta, Eastern, Pan Am, Piedmont, TWA, and United. Chalk's flies seaplanes from Florida to Paradise Island, Bimini, Cat Cay, and Walker's Cay (Abaco). Bahamasair, the national carrier, flies from several cities on the U.S. East Coast and connects Nassau with the Family Islands.

Charter flights are a popular way to get to the Bahamas. To make your own charter arrangements, contact private charter companies in major south Florida cities.

Perhaps the best buys in airfare come with complete vacation packages, which generally include round-trip airfare, hotel accommodations for a specified number of nights, and transfers between airport and hotel, including luggage handling. The following is a sampling of recently offered vacation packages. Prices are per person, double occupancy.

Lucayan Beach Resort, Grand Bahama, 7 nights. $549, including TWA airfare from/to Boston or New York. $30–$75 additional airfare from 22 other U.S. cities. A three-night package at the same hotel: $359. Mid-April to mid-December.

Sheraton Grand Hotel, Paradise Island, 7 nights. $549–$589, including Delta airfare from/to New York or Newark. Additional fare from/to other U.S. cities. Two nights at the same hotel: $319–$329. Mid-April to mid-

December. Lowest prices apply for most of June, September, and October.

Nassau Beach Hotel, Nassau, 7 nights. $619–$769, including Pan Am airfare from/to New York. Three nights: $389–$459. Winter rate (January).

Nassau Beach Hotel, Nassau, 7 nights. $682–$710, including Piedmont airfare from/to any of 55 U.S. cities. Three nights: $394–$414. Winter rate (January).

Stella Maris Inn honeymoon or *Out Island Adventure,* Long Island, 5 nights. $659, including arranged airfare from/to Fort Lauderdale. Mid-December through April.

Perhaps the biggest air transportation bargain is the day trip to Freeport. You can fly from Fort Lauderdale to Freeport and back on weekdays for as little as $59 (off-season rate). It's a 20-minute Braniff flight. The price, which never goes higher than $99 (for weekend travel during high season), includes round-trip airport transfers to the Bahamas Princess Resort and Casino, a buffet lunch, and casino admission.

Cruises. Half of all visitors to the Bahamas now arrive on cruise ships. The vessels that visit most often include the following:

- *Britanis,* Chandris Fantasy Cruises, from Miami (weekly).
- *Carnivale,* Carnival Cruise Lines, from Miami (twice weekly).
- *Costa Riviera,* Costa Cruises, from Fort Lauderdale (weekly).
- *Dolphin IV,* Dolphin Cruises, from Miami (twice weekly).
- *Emerald Seas,* Admiral Cruise Lines, from Miami (twice weekly).
- *Fairsky,* Sitmar Cruises, from Fort Lauderdale (ten-night cruises, several departures during the year).
- *Fairwind,* Sitmar Cruises, from Fort Lauderdale (ten-night cruises, several departures during the year).
- *Galileo,* Chandris Fantasy Cruises, from Miami (weekly).
- *Homeric,* Home Lines, from Fort Lauderdale (weekly).
- *Jubilee,* Carnival Cruise Lines, from Miami (weekly).
- *Mardi Gras,* Carnival Cruise Lines, from Fort Lauderdale (twice weekly).
- *Mermoz,* Paquet French Cruises, from Tampa (weekly).
- *Rotterdam,* Holland America Line, from Fort Lauderdale (weekly).

- *Starship Oceanic,* Premier Cruise Lines, from Port Canaveral (twice weekly).
- *Starship Royale,* Premier Cruise Lines, from Port Canaveral (twice weekly).
- *Sunward II,* Norwegian Caribbean Lines, from Miami (twice weekly).

ENTRY

No passport is required to visit the Bahamas if you are a U.S., Canadian, or British citizen planning to stay no longer than three weeks. You need proof of citizenship, however, and a birth certificate is preferred.

Hold onto the white immigration card that you're given right before you arrive in the Bahamas. When departure time comes, you won't be able to leave the country without it.

DEPARTURE

You'll pay a $5 departure tax (in either currency) when you check in for your flight home. U.S. customs is often handled in Nassau before you get on your flight, so be prepared by listing your purchases and their prices on the white card. Every U.S. citizen is allowed to return home with up to $400 worth of purchases from the Bahamas duty-free.

MONEY

If you are traveling with U.S. dollars, there's no need to exchange money or to visit a Bahamian bank at all. The Bahamian dollar and the U.S. dollar are almost exactly equal at press time. You may pay with either currency, and your change may come back in either—or in a combination of the two. If you still have Bahamian money at departure time, exchange it at the Nassau airport's Royal Bank of Canada branch.

Most hotels, restaurants, and stores accept major credit cards, particularly American Express, MasterCard, and Visa; Diners Club and Carte Blanche are widely accepted, too. You can cash traveler's checks at your hotel's front desk.

TIPS FOR BRITISH VISITORS

Government Tourist Office. For information on the Bahamas, call or write the Bahamas Tourist Office, 10 Chesterfield St., London W1A 8AH (tel. 01/629–0587).

Passports and Visas. Visitors from Britain do not need passports for visits of less than three weeks; a birth certificate or similar form of identification is sufficient. But remember that you will need a passport to return to Britain. Visas are not required.

Customs & Duties. Returning to Britain you may bring home: (1) 200 cigarettes or 100 cigarillos or 50 cigars or 250 grams of tobacco; (2) two liters of table wine with additional allowances for (a) one liter of alcohol over 22° by volume, or (b) two liters of alcohol under 22° by volume (38.8° proof, most spirits), or (c) two more liters of table wine; and (3) 50 grams of perfume and ¼ liter of toilet water, and (4) other goods up to a value of £32.

Insurance. We strongly recommend that you insure yourself to cover health, loss of luggage (if not already covered in an existing homeowner's policy you may have), trip cancellation, and motoring mishaps while you are in the Bahamas. Europ Assistance, 252 High St., Croydon CRO 1NF (tel. 01/680–1234), offers an excellent service.

Tour Operators. Package tours to the Bahamas undoubtedly offer the best value for money. Here is a selection of companies offering such packages; check with your travel agent for details.

Albany Travel (Manchester) Ltd., 190 Deansgate, Manchester M3 3WD (tel. 061/833–0202).

Dream Islands of the World, 5 Charterhouse Bldgs., Goswell Rd., London EC1M 7AN (tel. 01/253–2662).

Kuoni Travel, Kuoni House, Dorking, Surrey RH5 4AZ (tel. 01/0306–885044). Seven-night vacations in an apartment hotel, from £508 per person, or from £690 in a luxury hotel, complete with 18-hole golf course, swimming pool, and tennis courts.

Harlequin Holidays Ltd., 146 West St., Sheffield S1 4ES (tel. 0742/750508), specialize in tailor-made vacations to Nassau, Exuma, and Abaco. Prices are quoted on request.

Sovereign Worldwide, Trafalgar House, 2 Chalk Hill Rd., London W6 8DN (tel. 01/748–4495), offers seven nights from £599. There are also two-weeks-for-the-price-of-one and three-weeks-for-the-price-of-two offers available.

Tradewinds Faraway Holidays, Station House, 81–83 Fulham High St., London SW6 3JP (tel. 01/731–8000). Seven nights at a "superior" hotel from £588, at a "deluxe" from £648 per person. There are also extra free week options.

Airfares. If you're considering traveling to the Bahamas independently, you should explore the budget flight possibilities. APEX and other fares are offered by airlines at a considerable saving over the full price. At press time an APEX round-trip to Nassau cost in the region of £429.

NASSAU AND
PARADISE ISLAND

If you arrive in Nassau by cruise ship, you'll be deposited right by Rawson Square. That puts you in front of the government buildings and the statue of Queen Victoria, in the center of town and the Bay Street shopping.

If you arrive by plane, the Nassau airport will be your first glimpse of the Bahamas. It's a long, sunny walk from the plane to the terminal, but immigration and luggage pickup go quickly. You may be in your hotel room 45 minutes after you land.

The airport itself is surprisingly small when you consider that Nassau receives 700,000 foreign visitors by air every year. Whether you're coming, going, or laying over here, don't expect a great variety of activities. Actual offerings may change from time to time, but you're most likely to find a

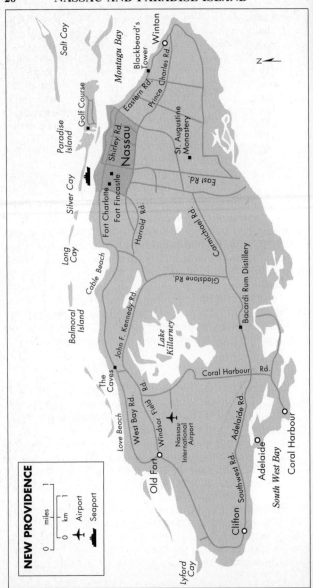

NEW PROVIDENCE

0   miles

0   km

✈ Airport

⚓ Seaport

Salt Cay

Montagu Bay

Blackbeard's Tower

Winton

Eastern Rd.

Prince Charles Rd.

Golf Course

Paradise Island

St. Augustine Monastery

Silver Cay

Shirley Rd.

Nassau

East Rd.

Fort Charlotte

Fort Fincastle

Long Cay

Harrold Rd.

Commercial Rd.

Cable Beach

Gladstone Rd.

Bacardi Rum Distillery

Balmoral Island

John F. Kennedy Rd.

Lake Killarney

The Caves

Coral Harbour Rd.

Love Beach

West Bay Rd.

Windsor Field Rd.

Adelaide Rd.

Nassau International Airport

Southwest Rd.

Adelaide

South West Bay

Coral Harbour

Old Fort

Clifton

Lyford Cay

newsstand, a liquor store, a coffee shop, a perfume counter, and small branches of the post office and bank.

If you're leaving or arriving on a weekend, don't expect to find full services here. Some services may be open only Monday through Friday during normal business hours.

If you're part of a tour group, your transportation to the hotel probably will be arranged, via minibus. Otherwise you'll have to take a taxi, which you'll find just outside the terminal.

All Nassau cabs are required to have meters in good working order, but no watchdog rides along to be sure they're used. No problem; just be sure to settle on a rate *before* the cab pulls away.

You may prefer to rent a car. If you plan to do a lot of moving around during your stay, it will be a good idea to contact Avis, Budget, Hertz, National, or one of the local rental firms. You'll find car rental counters both at the airport and at some hotels. At press time, rates start at about $45 per day and $250 per week, both with unlimited mileage. It may not turn out to be a lot cheaper than cabbing, but at least you'll know ahead of time what you're spending.

Nassau's hotel district is on Cable Beach, between the airport and the city. The name refers to the telegraph cable laid there in 1892 from Jupiter, Florida, to the Bahamas, but the area has a somewhat more glamorous history. As early as 1809, and throughout the 19th and early 20th centuries, horse racing was the leisure-time attraction in this part of town. Pineapple plantations took over the area later. Then the first luxury beach resorts began to be built after World War II.

Although a number of those older hotels still stand, along with apartment hotels, condominiums, and guest houses, most visitors find themselves in one of the four largest and most modern Cable Beach hotels.

The **Cable Beach Hotel,** open since 1983, is by far the glitziest. Red brick terraces dotted with dramatic fountains lead to the entry. The lobby, with its plush, dark green furniture, seems palatial; modern staircases lead up to a bar and down to a restaurant.

The hallway to your right will take you to the casino and conference center, but not without your passing an arcade of modern shops on both sides. They include a branch of Androsia for resort wear, the Chez Mizpah boutique for same, two jewelry stores, a liquor store, a leather goods shop, a large beauty salon, a florist, a photo shop, and a drugstore. One nice thing about being in the casino hotel is that everything is open late; most shops don't close till 10 or 11 P.M.

Convention business is strong throughout the year at the Cable Beach, so the lobby is often dominated by mountains of suitcases signaling group arrivals and departures. There also appear to be plenty of unattached guests around, both male and female. Nowhere is that more obvious than at the pool/beach area, where you might see a man in a three-piece business suit standing in the sand to chat with a bikini-clad woman stretched out on a chaise.

You can take a private elevator to this area, which feels like a resort in itself. There are man-made rock grottos with waterfalls (including at least one that you can stand under), lots of footbridges, plus little wooden walkways and landscaped greenery near the large pool, where an amplified steel band is almost always playing.

The beach is clean and white but narrow, with a small area roped off for swimmers. There are separate oceanside bars for food, drink, and water sports. A large patio has frosted glass tables, aqua beach chairs, off-white umbrellas, and even thatched-roof gazebos for those who want to eat, drink, and ocean-gaze in comfortable shade. The poolside bathrooms have showers, a great convenience for sand-and-salt-caked swimmers.

The rooms ($160–$220 double) are among the island's most elegant, about 19 by 13 feet with plush carpet, two double beds with high bamboo headboards, chintz draperies, and a small balcony. Bathrooms have marble vanities, separate dressing areas, closets with mirrored sliding doors, complimentary shampoos and shower gels, and plugs for your hair dryer and shaver in all the right places. And there's cable TV, air-conditioning, and a touch-tone phone.

Available sports include parasailing, boating, scuba diving, deep-sea fishing, water-skiing, and table tennis. The hotel's 9,000-square-foot sports center is just across the street. Open from 8 A.M. to 10 P.M. every day, it has tennis, squash, and racquetball courts in addition to an exercise room (exercise classes are free to guests). The 18-hole golf course is nearby.

The 700-room Cable Beach gives you a choice of 11 different places to eat or drink; the most elegant is the fourth-floor Regency Room for Continental cuisine by candlelight. The Riviera Room, a bit more casual, is the place for steaks and seafood. Both are open for dinner only. The informal King Conch Cafe, opening onto the terrace, is open 24 hours a day.

Cable Beach Hotel, c/o Wyndham Hotel Company, 5775 N.W. 11th Street, Miami, FL 33126. (305) 262–1397 or (800) 822–4200.

The **Nassau Beach Hotel,** next door, had its heyday in the late 1950s and early 1960s when the Beatles, Brigitte Bardot, and other celebrities of the era stayed here. Thanks to a recent multimillion-dollar renovation, it still holds its own among the big three. Its facade is all new brick, white louvers, and sparkling new "old-fashioned" gas lanterns on the exterior walls.

The guests, mostly couples, range in age from post-pubescent newlyweds to retirees, with a slight emphasis on the latter. If you need an indication that the crowd is somewhat older here, take note that the T-shirts on sale inside say, "My grandma and grandpa went to the Bahamas, and all I got was this lousy T-shirt."

This is a very pleasant hotel, with a front desk staff friendlier than most in this part of the Bahamas, and 425 attractively decorated guest rooms, every one with an ocean view. Typical decor includes an abstract design bedspread in tones of rust, beige, and off-white, casual white furniture with mocha accents, and white louvered doors. Sliding glass doors lead to a triangular balcony large enough for two chairs and a tiny table. The bath and dressing room have double basins, good for a couple trying to get ready at the same time. There's a phone, air-conditioning, room service, hair dryers, color TV, and more storage space than you could ever need.

The hotel has three wings, built at different times, with slightly larger rooms in the "new" wing (circa 1969). The newly designated private concierge section is called the Palm

Club. Double room rates range from $125 to $240, with Palm Club rooms at the high end of the scale.

The place to swim is the pool, surrounded by off-white beach umbrellas with muted pastel stripes and chaises with matching cushions. The 3,000-foot stretch of beach is fine for sunning, but the area roped off for swimming is barely large enough to get wet.

All the water sports you could want are right here: windsurfing, sailing, snorkeling, paddleboating, parasailing, water-skiing, fishing, and rides in a glass-bottom boat. The tennis courts are lighted for night play, and other organized activities range from volleyball to bingo and backgammon.

The Nassau Beach was the first hotel in town to open a nouvelle cuisine restaurant, and it has continued to move with the food-trend times. Since its most recent renovation, wining and dining choices include Pineapple Place (for French food by candlelight and plantation-house decor), the Beef Cellar (where you may grill your own steak), and the Out Island Bar.

Hotel shops include a liquor store, a beauty salon, and a small resort wear boutique.

Nassau Beach Hotel National Sales Office, 500 Deer Run, Miami, FL 33166. (305) 871–1830, (800) 223–5672, or (809) 327–7711.

Wyndham's **Ambassador Beach Hotel** has just undergone an extensive three-year refurbishment in which all rooms got new floor coverings, wallpaper, and furniture without the hotel's undergoing structural changes. The newly redecorated rooms ($120–$160, single or double) all have balcony, telephone, and cable TV.

The new restaurant is the Pasta Kitchen, where you'll find homemade Italian specialties in an intimate, oak-paneled setting. Among the carryovers from prerenovation days are the Flamingo Café dining room, the Bunday Bar & Grill, and the Pelican Bar and Game Room with its oversize TV screen, dart boards, and games tables.

Ambassador Beach Hotel, c/o Wyndham Hotel Company, 5775 N.W. 11th Street, Miami, FL 33126. (800) 822–4200 or (305) 262–1397.

The **Royal Bahamian** began life in the 1940s as a private club (the Balmoral), then became a public hotel in 1967 and was soon outdone by its bigger, more modern neighbors in Cable Beach.

It reopened in December 1984, after a $7-million renovation, as the Royal Bahamian to mostly rave reviews. Most rooms ($145–$215) are in the six-story manor house; the rest are in villas (up to $1,250 per day for the three-bedroom suite). Rates include daytime tennis, entertainment every night, free transportation to the Cable Beach Casino, use of the fitness center (only massages and mud baths cost extra), and aerobics classes.

Haute cuisine is the fare at Baccarat's, simpler meals at Café Royale.

The Royal Bahamian, c/o Wyndham Hotel Company, 5775 N.W. 11th Street, Miami, FL 33126. (800) 822–4200 or (305) 262–1397.

When you leave the Cable Beach area, it will probably be for your first shopping expedition downtown. Some hotels offer free transportation at least twice a day. Otherwise, you can take a taxi or meet the Bahamians by taking a public "bus."

The buses, which are vans with 10 to 20 seats, stop in front of the Cable Beach hotels and take you straight into the Bay Street shopping area. Remember, they drive on the left here, so when you are going downtown, wait on the same side of the street the hotels are on.

It's interesting to see the scenery and the glimpses of non-tourist Nassau in between, and to play musical chairs (as the Bahamians politely do for each other) as people get on and off the vehicle. The buses will stop to pick you up almost anywhere. Of course, if you're agile, you can jump on board a moving bus, streetcar-style. If not, a good place to get one to stop is right in front of the Sheraton.

The **Sheraton British Colonial** is a downtown landmark that in recent years has looked grander from the outside than it really is. Built in the 1920s, it still stands elegantly with its apple-green canopy and pink facade. Inside, there are sometimes noisy tour groups checking in and out, and long corridors upstairs lead to rooms decorated in slightly upscale motel style. We have received many complaints about this hotel from disappointed guests, but a recent renovation greatly improved at least some of the rooms here. If shopping is one of your highest priorities, the location may be worth the risk. Like any good resort hotel, the Sheraton has a pool, a beach, and a waterside bar. Rooms are $109–$169, single or double.

If you want to sightsee downtown, stroll to Rawson Square and hire a horse-drawn carriage. Your horse will trot along the old sections of Nassau, directly behind the bustling shopping area, where old homes (some of them turned into fine restaurants like Graycliff and Buena Vista) are located.

If you'd prefer a wider range of sightseeing, hire a taxi driver to show you around. You've already seen Prince George Dock and the statue of Queen Victoria downtown; that was Parliament Square. Nearby you'll find the 126-foot water tower, tiny Fort Fincastle, and the queen's staircase.

Sights west of town include Fort Charlotte (built in 1798 and large enough for guided tours) and the upper-crust residential areas of Highland Park, Prospect Ridge, and Skyline Heights.

Fort Montagu, on the other side of the island of New Providence, is a history lesson of two eras. The fort is from the early 1700s; the now abandoned hotel of the same name was *the* beach hotel in the 1940s.

Or you can see all of the above on a two-hour guided city and country tour. A four-hour city tour adds the show at Seafloor Aquarium and a Bahamian lunch. Even if you're sightseeing on your own, you can drop by the aquarium for the show, in which trained sea lions and dolphins perform every two hours.

Finding interesting tours—from the sightseeing variety to full-day sailing trips or Out Island picnics—is no problem. Your hotel's tour desk will be piled high with brochures, and staff members will be eager to book you on one or more outings.

One of the most popular is aboard the *Nautilus,* a 97-foot glass-bottom showboat that makes five two-hour cruises per day. Underwater attractions include coral reefs, tropical fish, and even a shipwreck. Then there's the all day Treasure Island trip, a leisurely cruise that drops you off for hours of swimming, sunning, snorkeling, and Bahamian eating, far from the Nassau crowds. If you want to see more of the Bahamas, there are day trips to Freeport and to Harbour Island (off Eleuthera).

PARADISE ISLAND

Cross the toll bridge on the northeastern side of Nassau, and you've arrived in what may be the most active, self-contained resort island in the world: Paradise Island. Joseph Lynch (as in Merrill, Lynch) lived here before World War II, when it was still called Hog Island. Then the Swedish industrialist Axel Wenner-Gren took over. But development really began in the 1960s, when the company that is now Resorts International became involved.

The one problem you may have with Paradise Island is keeping the names straight. Resorts International owns, among other properties, the Paradise Island Resort & Casino, which includes the Britannia Towers Hotel, the Paradise Towers Hotel (the two have a total of 1,100 rooms), and the casino that connects them.

The **Britannia Towers** is the more elegant hotel, but not dramatically so. The gleaming lobby, with its marble front desk and columns, brass chandeliers, and light blue walls, is a combination of modern and casual decor. And it is almost always filled with people, activity, and the hum of many voices. Convention groups and dedicated gamblers make up a big part of the clientele.

At the Britannia, you have four choices of where to stay. The North Tower ($165–$300, single or double), just six years old, has attractive, identically furnished rooms throughout. Among the furnishings are blue carpets, bedspreads in a handsome blue seashell-and-net print, closets with sliding glass doors, a minifridge, and a wallpapered bath with all the amenities.

Within the North Tower, the Paradise Concierge Floors (floors 9–12) are a key club that offers private check-in, complimentary Continental breakfast in a private 12th-floor room, a rooftop sundeck with hot tub, plus other extras. A typical Concierge Floor guest room features two double beds

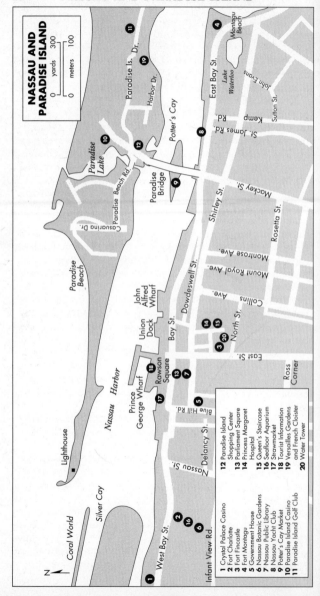

NASSAU AND PARADISE ISLAND

yards 300
meters 100

N

1 Crystal Palace Casino
2 Fort Charlotte
3 Fort Fincastle
4 Fort Montagu
5 Government House
6 Nassau Botanic Gardens
7 Nassau Public Library
8 Nassau Yacht Club
9 Potter's Cay Market
10 Paradise Island Casino
11 Paradise Island Golf Club
12 Paradise Island Shopping Center
13 Parliament Square
14 Princess Margaret Hospital
15 Queen's Staircase
16 Seafloor Aquarium
17 Strawmarket
18 Tourist Information
19 Versailles Gardens and French Cloister
20 Water Tower

Coral World
Silver Cay
Lighthouse
Nassau Harbor
Paradise Beach
Paradise Lake

Paradise Is. Dr.
Harbor Dr.
Paradise Beach Rd.
Casuarina Dr.

East Bay St.
Montagu Beach
Lake Waterloo
John Evans
Sutton St.

Kemp Rd.
St. James Rd.
Potter's Cay
Paradise Bridge
Shirley St.
Mackey St.
Montrose Ave.
Mount Royal Ave.
Collins Ave.
Rosetta St.
North St.
East St.
Dowdeswell St.
Bay St.
John Alfred Wharf
Union Dock
Prince George Wharf
Rawson Square
Blue Hill Rd.
Delancy St.
Nassau St.
West Bay St.
Infant View Rd.
Ross Corner

with black-and-white print spreads, a mirrored wall, rose-colored carpet and chairs, sliding glass doors leading to a small balcony, and an attractive bath with a large marble vanity (and little luxuries like complimentary shampoos and conditioners). Rates are slightly higher ($330, single or double) than those at the rest of the North Tower.

Rooms in the hotel's South Tower (also $165–$300, single or double) are larger, if not quite as modern or as luxuriously furnished. Decor includes navy floral print spreads, navy carpet, wallpapered bathroom with phone and fridge, plus balcony. The South Tower was good enough for Howard Hughes, and you can rent his three-bedroom suite (#924, #925, and #926) or any part thereof.

The Britannia also has five villas, each with 16 units. There are no kitchen facilities here. The attraction is being able to walk out your door in the morning and immediately be by the pool or beach. There is only one oceanfront villa, and it costs no more than the others. Sizes range from a standard room layout ($115, single or double) to a three-bedroom villa with private pool ($360, single, double, or triple). A minimum three-night stay is required for the villas only.

This luxury hotel has what may be the best health club in the Bahamas. The room with hot tub and exercise equipment isn't huge, but it's mirrored, modern, and very attractive. Sauna and massage are available.

The Paradise Island Resort & Casino is an all-indoor world if you want it to be. You can walk from the Britannia lobby through an arcade of shops and elegant restaurants into the casino, and from the casino step into the Paradise Towers lobby.

Shops include branches of Mademoiselle (for women's clothes) and Colombian Emeralds, a men's boutique, plus a drugstore and a liquor store.

Then you arrive in Birdcage Walk, which is just a circular stopping place with a fountain and a round, rust-striped velvet banquette for drinking, resting your feet, or waiting for your dinner date. Several of the resort's gourmet restaurants surround it.

The restaurants include Villa d'Este, for Italian specialties ranging from veal to pasta; Coyaba, for Szechuan and Polynesian dishes; and the terribly tasteful, somewhat masculine Bahamian Club for Continental and British dishes.

The casino, which is active 24 hours a day, is just ahead. When you're in the mood for breakfast at two in the afternoon or a midnight snack at two in the morning, there's the Café Casino. It keeps gamblers' hours, 11 A.M. to 2 A.M. every day.

If your winnings are impressive, you can stop in the Crystal Cave and buy a beautiful piece of Lalique or Waterford to celebrate. Then you're on the red carpet walkway into the Paradise Towers lobby, where you can drop into a branch of Greenfire Emeralds if you have any money left.

Paradise Towers' lobby has been completely redone in a tropical-atrium style, complete with fountains and foliage. Guest rooms ($165–$300, single or double) are decorated exactly like those in the Britannia's North Tower.

At this writing, dining choices just off the lobby include Gulfstream for seafood specialties and Seagrapes for informal meals—breakfast, lunch, or dinner. The resort's very casual Boathouse restaurant and its very French Café Martinique are across the street from the Britannia.

The two-hotel resort has two pools, 12 tennis courts, an 18-hole golf course, horseback riding, and a parcourse jogging trail. The three-mile stretch of beach allows for all water sports, including snorkeling, scuba diving, sunfish sailing, water-skiing, parasailing, windsurfing, and paddleboating.

But the resort doesn't want you to miss the sights. There's a free 45-minute bus tour of Paradise Island twice a day, free bus service to Nassau's Rawson Square where you can shop, and water taxi service to downtown Nassau for the same purpose.

Paradise Island Resort & Casino, Paradise Island, Bahamas. (800) 321–3000 or (305) 895–2922.

The **Sheraton Grand Hotel,** next door, is still the new kid on the block and very stiff competition for the well-established hotels. The Grand is certainly the most attractive—and possibly the most courteous—hotel on Paradise Island.

If it's the newest golden boy in the Paradise Island hotel industry, it lives up to its name. The understated, atrium-like lobby is filled with gleaming brass, rose colored marble, golden-brown tile floors, light golden wood columns, lots of lush greenery around the fountain, and just a touch of red carpet. There are brown sofas, high-back wicker chairs in the sitting areas, and a handsome lobby bar.

Almost everything here lives up to top aesthetic standards. Le Paon, the island's most fashionable disco, and Julie's, one of the most elegant restaurants here, are as beautifully decorated as they are popular. Even the Verandah, the casual restaurant for breakfast, lunch, and dinner, is much more special than the usual coffeeshop setting. It's an attractive series of rooms with polished bamboo, off-white cushions, and ocean views. Only the hotel's pool area is undistinguished, and the beach makes up for it.

All guest rooms ($150–$330, single or double) have ocean views. The decor includes double beds with confetti-pattern spreads, floral print dust ruffles, off-white draperies, sliding glass doors leading to a small balcony, and a white louvered double closet with an unstocked fridge inside. The wallpapered baths have large marble vanities and built-in hair dryers. And there's satellite TV, phone, and air-conditioning.

The 12th floor has been designated the Grand Tier (all rooms $275). Guests here have their own concierge, complimentary Continental breakfast, complimentary afternoon wine and cheese, and such little perks as turndown service and toiletries.

Once, if you had saved *lots* of money for your vacation, you could rent the Grand's penthouse suite for $11,000 a day. This four-bedroom wonder has its own security desk, an almost-nine-foot-long marble bathtub with ocean view in the master bath, gold and marble fixtures, and a hot tub on the living room balcony. Now there are reports that it has been sold, and unless the owner is willing to rent it out privately, you'll have to settle for accommodations with a bit less square footage.

Sports at the Grand include tennis (four courts), parasailing, windsurfing, and all water sports, which you can schedule at the poolside center. The Paradise Island golf course is nearby.

Lobby shops include branches of Androsia, a liquor store, a florist, and a drugstore.

The Sheraton Grand Hotel, Paradise Island, Bahamas. (800) 327-4551 or (809) 326-2011.

The Ocean Club, although a Resorts International property, is as different from the company's two big hotels as night is from day. Set apart from the island bustle, closer to the Versailles Gardens than anything else, this was once the estate of the A&P heir Huntington Hartford; a feeling of privacy (not to mention a touch of elitism) remains. There's something more relaxed about this 70-room hotel than its neighbors, too; its PR people like to call it an Out Island atmosphere on Paradise Island.

The people who come here include many New Yorkers, a number of Europeans, and a sprinkling of tennis buffs. They pull into a curving driveway, enter what appears to be a rather grand old home, and sip rum punch while checking in at an antique writing desk. (The night before checkout, the bill will be delivered to the room and later picked up by a concierge.)

Rooms ($150-$350, single or double) and suites ($550-$600, single or double) overlook the central courtyard, where guests take most of their meals at white wrought-iron chairs under scalloped white beach umbrellas, around a cross-shaped pool and fountain surrounded by palms, schefflera, and other greenery.

All guest rooms boast minibars, bathroom phone extensions, and amenities from terry-cloth robes to bath gels and shampoos. The baths are probably the most luxurious in the Bahamas, with green jungle-leaf wallpaper, dark green tile floors, double basin, makeup stool, toiletries, and a separate WC with bidet. Almost all the guest rooms have balconies.

If you're looking for total privacy, a villa ($750 for two to four people) with a high-walled patio could be the best choice. You get a living room with fireplace and high pine ceilings, two elegant bedrooms and baths, and a kitchenette. Every villa but one has its own hot tub.

The villas are across the way, near the huge pool, nine tennis courts, tennis shop, drugstore, and outdoor lunch restaurant. The Ocean Club's only indoor dining room is used primarily in bad weather. Even afternoon tea is served in the Courtyard Terrace gardens ($7.50, 3:30-5:30 P.M.).

The real attraction is the ocean. Guests go down wooden steps, stop at the bar for a drink, a big yellow towel, or both, then continue to the clean, attractive (but slightly sloping) private beach. The water is very clear, and guests can reassure themselves that they made the right choice by simply glancing down the way to the more crowded hotel beaches beyond. All the usual water sports can be arranged here too.

Ocean Club, Paradise Island, Bahamas. (800) 321–3000 or (809) 326–2501.

Club Med, on the other side of Paradise Island, is just as much a world of its own. But oh, what a difference in the mood!

At the front gate things seem sedate enough. But stroll through the grounds to the bar overlooking the harbor, and you can be almost overwhelmed by the party mood. The friendliness seems quite genuine. The theme song, "Give Me Your Heart," can be heard on the PA system, and guests are singing and dancing along.

Club Med is and always has been a one-of-a-kind resort that creates its own environment, taking on only as much of a country or an island's character as the natural surroundings provide. Were it not for the beach here and the year-round sun, you could be almost anywhere.

Some of this particular club's acquired assets are the island's most gorgeous stretch of crescent-shaped beach, spectacular grounds, and what may be the largest and best pool at any Bahamian resort. The estate on which the club is built belonged to an Olympic swimmer, and she built the pool for her own practice sessions!

The guest register seems to be evenly divided between couples and singles, with a sprinkling of Europeans among the predominantly U.S. crowd. Although a certain amount of topless sunbathing takes place here, Club Med is eager to shed its overly sexy image and is concentrating on sports activities more than ever before.

Tennis is the specialty at this club. You can take advantage of the Intensive Tennis program, which gives you three hours of lessons per day (always with the same instructor) plus hours of tennis-related activities. They include watching video replays of your classes, ball-machine practice, tennis films, and special exercises for limbering up.

If you know John McEnroe only from his TV commercials and think Martina Navratilova is a Russian ballerina, don't let that stop you from visiting this Club Med. Many non-tennis players manage to have a fine time without ever picking up a racket.

Windsurfing is the second most popular sport here. The other choices of activities (all included in your vacation price) include sailing, snorkeling, archery, yoga, calisthenics, and volleyball.

A one-week winter vacation costs $700–$1,150 plus airfare (the bargain rates are in January and early February). That includes three meals a day and free wine with every meal except breakfast. This is no small benefit, for Club Med's varied buffets are almost frightening in scope. Many a first-time guest has put his napkin on the table after a satisfying plateful, only to learn that what he had finished were merely the appetizers. The main courses are set up on another terrace nearby.

Club Med rooms are all doubles. If you don't bring a roommate, they'll find you one. The club's rooms are not renowned for their luxury or size: A typical room has twin beds and a no-frills bath with shower, no TV or room service, but then no one here spends much time lolling around the room. The disco is always open till 3 A.M. or so.

Club Med Sales and Information Center, 40 West 57th Street, New York, NY 10019. (800) 528-3100.

The club's nearest neighbor is the **Yoga Retreat,** effectively isolated from the rest of Paradise Island. You can get there by ferry from Nassau or, if you have the energy, you can sneak in the back door by walking along the beach. There are 38 rooms and "beach huts" ($35–$46 double).

The dining room serves vegetarian meals only. Although the emphasis here is on yoga, other activities (including tennis and snorkeling) are available, and there's a good beach. This is a very casual place—all the better for winding down and coming home rejuvenated, both physically and mentally.

Yoga Retreat, Box N-7550, Nassau, Bahamas, (809) 326-2902. No credit cards are accepted.

Paradise Paradise, on the other side of Club Med, has changed hands and names several times in the last few years. It now belongs to Resorts International again, and it has undergone major refurbishment.

The attractive front lawn is still dotted with palm trees and the pool is palm lined. There was no need to improve the beach, which rivals Club Med's as the best on the island. All 100 redecorated guest rooms have terraces and satellite TV. A hotel special offers water sports, tennis, bicycling, and aerobics. Paradise Pavillion, the hotel's new restaurant, boasts a very affordable menu.

This place has always drawn one of the younger crowds in this area, many of them in their 20s, perhaps because of the very casual atmosphere and the somewhat lower rates ($125–$185, single or double).

Paradise Paradise, Paradise Island, Bahamas. (800) 321–3000.

The **Holiday Inn** is the last hotel on this side (northwest) of the island, and the pool area is its claim to fame. Despite a private cove, the beach isn't the best in the area, yet the huge curving pool more than makes up for it. It snakes around a large deck, dotted with yellow chaises. And there are little footbridges over the pool to and from the thatched-roof snack bar.

This is an 18-floor high rise of soft yellow stucco, with rows of white iron balconies. The lobby is dramatic, if not sparkling new, with floor-to-ceiling windows (those ceilings are very high), rust-colored sectional sofas, wicker chairs with modern print cushions, tile floors with rust-colored carpets, and huge floral murals.

As you enter, facing the bar, you'll see an all-American crowd of all ages, probably with their Coke and 7-Up cans on the tables.

Neptune's Table, the lobby-level seafood restaurant, offers entrees from jackfish to *vol au vent,* with English trifle for dessert.

An arcade of shops in the rear lobby includes a resort-wear shop (heavy on the Androsia), a small jewelry store, a good drugstore, and a video arcade frequented by local teenagers.

Holiday Inn sports include tennis, minigolf, and all the usual water sports.

Rooms ($125–$185 double) are attractive, with carpeting, phones, balconies, and all the familiar comforts you'd expect here.

Holiday Inn, Paradise Island Beach Resort, Box 6214, Nassau, Bahamas. (809) 326–2101.

You can see **Loews Harbour Cove** from Nassau. It stands alone on Paradise Island's southeastern shore, a tall, modern, white hotel with its own special view of the Nassau harbor.

If the beach matters to you, don't stay here; this beach is a narrow sloping strip of beige sand facing the harbor. But the pool is just fine, and here is one of the Bahamas' very few swim-up bars. That is, you can enter the section of the pool adjacent to the drink and snack bar, sit on a partially submerged bar stool (water will be over your knees), order your drink, and sip it. Wherever you choose to roost, you can watch the Chalk's sea planes take off and land on the water all day.

The lobby is attractive and almost intimate, with rose-pink marble floors, huge potted plants, and recessed lighting. The furniture is a combination of wicker, solid and floral print green fabrics, and wine-red accents. The three lobby shops are branches of Mademoiselle and Colombian Emeralds, plus a combination newsstand and drugstore.

The 250 guest rooms ($125–$165, single or double) are sunny and spacious. A typical room has yellow floral print bedspreads, green carpeting, closets with mirrored sliding doors, a framed print that picks up the decor's sunny colors, and a wallpapered bath. Other features are color TV, radio, digital alarm clocks, air-conditioning, and a private phone.

Sports include tennis (two courts, lighted for night play), scuba, snorkeling, sailing, and all of the other usual water sports, plus shuffleboard, paddle tennis, and volleyball. Theme parties (Tuesday night is the Pig Roast Party, complete with fire dance) and special demonstrations are scheduled several days a week. When guests are ready for a change of scenery, it's a short walk to the Paradise Village Shopping Center. The free water taxi can take you right across the harbor to Nassau.

Loews Harbour Cove, Paradise Island, Bahamas. (809) 326–2563.

Paradise Island is no paradise for sightseers and history buffs. Almost everything here is new and/or part of a hotel complex. Yet every visitor should see the Versailles Gardens, the 14th-century cloister reconstructed stone by stone and set in a garden near the Ocean Club. You can thank Huntington Hartford for bringing it over from France.

The 18-hole Paradise Island Golf Club is impressive; it takes up the entire eastern end of the island. But if you're a golfer, you'll see that—as a matter of course.

GOOMBAY SUMMER

Summer 1989 marks the 18th year of Goombay summer. This celebration, originally intended to boost tourism in what was traditionally the slow season, has turned into an island-wide attraction in its own right. The four-month-long (June through September) summer festival offers a full calendar of social, cultural, and sporting events scheduled daily—and repeated weekly for visitors. Celebrations are especially intense in Nassau/Paradise Island, where each hotel sponsors its own beach parties, boat cruises, art fairs, and dances. In Nassau there are Junkanoo parades, Goombay music festivals, guided walking tours, and tea parties at Government House. Special golf, tennis, squash, and racquetball tournaments abound as well.

The wealth of activity only adds to the appeal of an off-season trip. Summer hotel rates are often 20 to 35 percent less than winter rates. At the Royal Bahamian, for instance, 1988 summer rates (April 17–December 14) started at $95, while the lowest winter rate was $145. On Paradise Island, the Ocean Club's rooms, which normally start at $150 in winter, rented for as little as $115 during most of spring, summer, and fall.

NASSAU DINING, SHOPPING, AND NIGHTLIFE

Many of your best Bahamian memories will have nothing to do with the beach. One advantage of vacationing in Nassau or Paradise Island is the variety of restaurants, shops, and entertainment available throughout the year.

There are French restaurants that serve caviar and foie gras; Italian restaurants that make their own pasta in the back room; and restaurants that have good old American hamburgers and french fries. Above all, there is Bahamian cuisine.

Grouper, frequently the fish of the day, is at its most "native" in the form of grouper fingers (a sort of home-fried fish sticks). Conch is on every menu in one form or another. Try

39

conch chowder for a starter, or conch salad for a light lunch. The traditional side dish is peas and rice, and that's delicious, too.

You'll find a restaurant on every corner, and you could eat very well without ever leaving your hotel's neighborhood. But the three restaurants that now compete for the title of Nassau's best all require a drive or a taxi ride downtown. Treating yourself to the very best is the thing to do in Nassau. It's worth the expense and the effort to get there; only in such places will you find the gracious service that once made this island the coveted retreat of the royal and the rich.

Warning: Ciguatera, a form of food poisoning caused by eating tropical reef fish such as sea bass, red snapper, and grouper, has been reported in the Bahamas. Though this form of poisoning is rare, the only way to avoid it entirely is to abstain from eating tropical reef fish.

THE ELEGANT THREE

Graycliff is a marvelous 240-year-old Georgian Colonial house with a history as intriguing as its menu. The Duke and Duchess of Windsor often played cards here when the house was still the Earl and Countess of Dudley's private home. And although notables from Onassis to the Beatles have enjoyed the hospitality since, the manager Enrico Garzaroli remembers Mick Jagger as his most likeable celebrity guest.

The tablecloths here are white crochet-work over solid pink linen, and the napkins are edged in old lace; the house even smells the way it should—there is just the softest hint of must. Guests look out through white louvers to the garden. Or they sit in the garden downstairs, relaxing in summer-striped cushioned chairs, listening to piano music or the fountain splash.

Graycliff is a hotel too, with 12 very elegant rooms renting for $140–$180 per day, but it is some distance from the beaches and better suited to a rock star in hiding than a vacationer in search of sun.

West Hill Street, opposite Government House, just outside the Nassau shopping district. Telephone 322–2796. Major credit cards accepted. Lunch and dinner.

Buena Vista, which wins many votes for the title of Nassau's finest restaurant, has been serving elegant meals for a quarter of a century. You'll enter through a black wrought-iron gate on Delancey Street, move down a small winding driveway, then walk under a maroon canopy into a grand old home. The large air-conditioned dining room, to your right, feels like one in a lovely country inn, accidentally transported from New England and set down in the islands. There's outdoor garden dining, too.

The service is gracious and impeccable, with a setting to match. Mustard tablecloths, wooden floors, hanging plants, and walls of old-fashioned paned windows looking out onto the lawn make for a certain country elegance. The entertainment consists of a male singer whose mood often changes from "Memories" to a double-entendre Bahamian song, then back again.

The wide menu includes Dover sole, steaks, lobster, chicken, and quail, with entree prices beginning at about $38. The set-price dinner (recently $32.50) includes a choice of soup or appetizer, a salad, and one of six daily specials with vegetables, then a choice of pastries from the fabulous dessert cart, plus coffee or tea.

Like Graycliff, Buena Vista is also an inn. But it is in the same neighborhood and not the best base for a sun-and-fun holiday.

Delancey Street, just outside the Nassau shopping district. Telephone 322–2811. Major credit cards accepted. Lunch and dinner. Closed Sundays.

Sun And . . . is yet another old Bahamian home turned into a Continental restaurant. All the way on the eastern side of the island, past the Nassau shopping district, it's well worth the drive. It has a former Graycliff chef and a fast-growing reputation as one of the town's top three dining spots.

Sun And . . . is formal yet not intimidating. There are flowers at your table and Queen Anne chairs. You enter through an archway then cross over a drawbridge. You can eat indoors or out, perhaps overlooking the greenery-banked pool.

The menu includes rack of lamb, chateaubriand (for two), and steaks, veal, and fish dishes. The table is yours for the evening, unlike the policy in some Nassau restaurants where you may be rushed to make way for the next seating.

Sun And . . . is on Lakeview Drive, off East Shirley Street. Telephone 323–1205. Major credit cards accepted. Dinner only, Tuesday through Sunday, 6:30–10 P.M. The restaurant is closed in August and September.

FINE HOTEL DINING

There are those nights when eight hours of lying in the sun has been all too much effort, and you can't bear to go further than downstairs for dinner. These could be the best choices, too, when you want the finest in food and service.

Julie's at the Sheraton Grand Hotel on Paradise Island started winning culinary stars almost from the day it opened. Low lights and romantic piano music welcome you to its three intimate rooms (there are two private dining rooms on the side).

The mood seems a bit of *la vie en rose,* with pink tablecloths under white lace, Louis XV-style chairs with pink floral print cushions, and pink banquettes along the walls. The food is decidedly French with a Continental accent, from *galantine de canard au poivre vert* or snails in puff pastry to flaming desserts like cherries jubilee and bananas Foster. Other entrees may include chicken Gismonda or *pres et maree* (that's surf and turf with béarnaise sauce).

Then there's the **Rotisserie.** The only beachfront restaurant in all of Nassau and Paradise Island, this lobby-level dining room features spit-roasted steaks, ribs, fowl, and game in season.

The Sheraton Grand Hotel, lobby level, Paradise Island. Telephone 326–2011. Dinner only, 7–10 P.M. seven days a week. Major credit cards accepted.

The Regency Room at the Cable Beach Hotel is very formal (there's a tendency to whisper your order) and in impeccable taste. Everything is burgundy, from the armchairs, plate trim, and napkins to the orchids in the crystal bud vases on each table. When you ask for a plain glass of water, you get Evian.

Such good taste is expensive, and it attracts as many of the hotel's business visitors as vacationers. Entrees range from baked red snapper in Creole sauce to pan-fried veal with morels and bourbon sauce. Appetizers range from the merely interesting—scallop mousse—to the extravagant—Beluga caviar or *terrine de foie gras de Strasbourg.*

Cable Beach Hotel, fourth floor. Telephone 327–6000. Major credit cards accepted. Dinner only.

Baccarat at the Royal Bahamian is the newest and perhaps the most elegant of hotel restaurants. The dining room is formal, with grand crystal chandeliers (from Baccarat, of course) and a wall of tall windows overlooking the pool and terrace. The same kind of formality appears on the menu, which juxtaposes classic entrees such as Dover sole, braised duckling, and rack of lamb with Caribbean-French surprises such as mosaic of grouper *fines herbes.*

Royal Bahamian Hotel, lobby level. Dinner only, 6–11 P.M. Telephone 327–6400. Major credit cards accepted.

Cafe Martinique on Paradise Island seems nothing like a hotel restaurant, but technically it's part of the Britannia Beach/Paradise Towers complex. The striped canopy and the setting here are formal, but the mood is not.

Whether you eat indoors (in red velvet chairs beneath one of the world's most gorgeous old chandeliers) or out (overlooking Paradise Lake and Nassau's lights across the way), you'll be treated to some of the area's liveliest and best old-fashioned dance music. The mood can switch from Gershwin to Dixieland jazz, depending on what the couples dancing in the moonlight request.

Dinner selections are just what you'd expect from a French cafe: *coq au vin,* beef Wellington, *langouste.* Grouper amandine, several veal dishes, and filet mignon are also on the menu. For an appetizer, you can blow the budget on caviar or foie gras, or you can keep it simple with melon or a shrimp cocktail. The service matches the mood: attentive, yet not overly solicitous.

Across the street and down the hill from the Grand Britannia, Paradise Island. Telephone 326–3000. Brunch and dinner. Major credit cards accepted.

Villa d'Este, just off the lobby of Paradise Island's Grand Britannia Hotel, is a grand high-ceilinged Italian restaurant that makes its own pasta. The setting is classical, with tufted, salmon-colored banquettes and Louis XV-style chairs, a gargantuan Murano-style (but wood!) chandelier, and a huge mural of its namesake, an estate outside Rome. Specialties include *saltimbocca, osso bucco,* and a variety of other veal dishes, plus seven kinds of pasta (available either as appetizer or entree). For the incurably sensible, there's a fruit basket on the dessert cart—right next to the vanilla and chocolate mousses.

Birdcage Walk, between the Grand Britannia lobby and the casino. Paradise Island. Telephone 326–3000. Dinner only. Major credit cards accepted.

HERE'S TO THE SHOPPERS WHO LUNCH

Virtually every visitor to Nassau spends at least half a day shopping on Bay Street, and eventually most of them get hungry. The interesting places for memorable lunches in downtown Nassau are tucked away on the side streets, so you must know where to look.

Roselawn is the loveliest. You know you've come to the right place when you realize that 80 percent of your fellow lunchers are local businessmen. This makes for an odd juxtaposition of shirts and ties at one table and Bermuda shorts at the next.

The Buena Vista people own Roselawn, and it shows. Beyond the rose-colored canopy you'll find an almost Mediterranean mood, with archways, carved wood doors, and ceramic tile floors. There's outdoor dining in the garden, too.

The service isn't quite up to Buena Vista standards, but neither are the prices. Hot and cold lunch entrees range from a very moderately priced BLT to a near perfect lobster salad. There are homemade pastas, too, and a lunch special that includes soup or salad, the entree of the day, fruit salad, and coffee.

At dinnertime Roselawn's main courses often include broiled chicken à l'américaine and a charcoal-broiled Bahamian lobster. You can still have the pastas, but they're more expensive at night.

Bank Lane, just past the police station (on your left), off Bay Street. Telephone 325–1018. Lunch (11:30–2:30) and dinner (6:30–10 P.M.). Major credit cards accepted. Closed Sundays.

The Green Shutters Inn is a popular casual spot for lunch, a touch of Old England in the middle of town. The pub atmosphere includes a fireplace, a dart board, and lots of dark wood. The menu is equally British, with roast beef and Yorkshire pudding and steak and kidney pie as well as local seafood specialties.

Parliament Street, off Bay Street at Rawson Square. Telephone 325-5702. Lunch (11:30–4) and dinner (6–10:30 P.M.). Major credit cards accepted.

The Terrace is a pleasant, unpretentious place for an outdoor lunch—the only true outdoor restaurant downtown. On a hot day you can be comfortable here under a beach umbrella, a shade tree, or both. (The small indoor dining room has the look of a Sears Roebuck layout for dinettes.)

Separated from the outside world by a stone wall, you can have a big tropical drink in a hurricane glass, then help yourself to the buffet ($6.95 for one trip to the serving table). Lunch ordered from the menu could be a steak, seafood, or chicken entree, a sandwich, or a Bahamian stew.

The Terrace serves dinner, too, offering such dishes as conch curry and surf and turf. Specialties include stone crab claws with garlic or mustard sauce, Papa Sam's chicken, and turtle pie. Round it off with English trifle or daiquiri pie for dessert. On Tuesday and Friday nights there's a Bahamian buffet and live music.

18 Parliament Street, outside the Parliament Hotel. Telephone 322-2836. Lunch (noon–4 P.M.) and dinner (6–10:30 P.M.). Major credit cards accepted.

The Cellar lives up to its name, a cool, dark place to stop for a beer or glass of wine on a hot shopping day. You can have a casual lunch, too, in the front room or on the garden patio.

The hearty selections include five kinds of pub lunches (perhaps the English pork pie and salad or the Frenchman's platter) plus such hot dishes as jambalaya, lasagna, and stuffed eggplant; you'll also find five kinds of quiche.

11 Charlotte Street, off Bay Street. Lunch only. AE and MC accepted for large bills only.

OUT-OF-THE-WAY

The Poop Deck is a casual, ketchup-bottle-on-the-table kind of place overlooking the water. The bar has a low-key nautical feel with lots of boating photos and a No Opium Smoking sign on the wall.

A good number of local people and boaters join tourists for relaxed outdoor dining here. Even at dinner the menu is unpretentious; chicken in the basket, burgers, grouper fingers, and the like.

The lunch menu is similar but cheaper, and everything comes with french fries or Bahamian peas and rice. This is a good spot for lunch when you've been sightseeing down this way. It's also a great choice when you want an inexpensive dinner with a view.

Go to East Bay Street, across from the Pilot House, east of the Paradise Island bridge. Lunch and dinner. Major credit cards accepted.

Captain Nemo's, another harborside restaurant specializing in seafood and steaks, is closer to town. Go for lunch. You'll find steaks, sandwiches, salads, quiches, and a couple of specials (they change every day—perhaps a choice of baked chicken or minced lobster on Tuesday, baked ham or chicken on Saturday). You can watch the Nautilus "surface submarine" tours and the ferry to the Yoga Retreat come and go as you eat.

Deveaux Street, four blocks east of Rawson Square. Telephone 325-2876. Lunch (noon–3 P.M.) and dinner (6–10 P.M.). Major credit cards accepted.

Traveller's Rest is still a good spot for a weekday lunch on your way to the airport or when you're exploring the area near Lyford Cay.

It's an unimpressive white stucco building with an orange roof, set in a grove of palm and sea grape trees, but its unpretentiousness has never bothered its celebrity and tourist clientele. Eat inside on a wooden bench beneath pink plank-shuttered windows and a motley assortment of art or on the patio at picnic tables. The view of blue-green sea is worth any discomfort from the heat, and a red Campari umbrella or the waving palm fronds above will help keep you cool.

Everybody orders from the blackboard menu, with its changing specials like breaded grouper fingers, conch chowder, pork chops, steamed conch, and curried chicken—all with spicy peas and rice. Lunch with a beer or glass of wine falls into the moderate price category.

Don't arrive for lunch before one, or you might find the place empty. And although the real action is on Sundays when there's live music, the consensus is that there may be a little too much action at times.

Bring your swimsuit. The small white-sand beach across the road is dotted with rocks to stretch out on, and the sea is often calm enough for swimming.

This is also a good spot to try if you have a mid-day layover at the airport. A short taxi ride will bring you here.

West Bay Street, near Gambier. Telephone 327–7633. Lunch and dinner. AE, V.

CASUAL DINNERS

Albrion's, one of Nettie Symonette's restaurants, is located at her Casuarinas Apartments on Cable Beach. The Bahamian/American dinner specialties here include Eleuthera chicken, Inagua pork chops, and Bimini snapper. The lunch menu has more casual offerings: hot dogs and cracked conch.

At any time of day the indoor setting is informal, with tile floors, ceiling fans, mustard yellow tablecloths, hanging plants, and local art. Most of the diners will have arrived by taxi from the nearby Cable Beach hotels.

Casuarinas Apartments, Cable Beach, west of the big hotels. Telephone 327–7921. Breakfast, lunch, and dinner. Major credit cards accepted.

Liz's Steak and Seafood Restaurant is the perfect spot for a late dinner before dancing the night away at the nearby Palace Disco.

It's a pretty little beige house with two floors of dining at brown-clothed tables with bentwood chairs, and an old-fashioned jukebox flashing away downstairs. Dinner entrees include lobster thermidor, grouper royal (with bananas, herbs, and chutney), scampi, T-bone steak, filet mignon, and surf and turf. At lunch, when you may find more local residents than tourists, there's a budget special—or a choice of steamed fish, conch, or chicken.

Elizabeth Avenue, off Bay Street. Telephone 322–4780. Lunch and dinner (till 2 A.M.). No dinner service on Mondays. Major credit cards accepted.

Da Vinci, a popular place for dinner, is just outside the Nassau shopping district. Both Italian and French cuisine are served, and the mood is formal enough to require jackets for the gentlemen.

West Bay Street, two doors west of the Sheraton. Telephone 322–2748. Dinner only, 7–11 P.M. Major credit cards accepted.

SHOPPING

There's no trick to shopping for souvenirs, gifts, and special bargains in Nassau. The stores are all in one area on Bay and its side streets. The salespeople are relatively polite, and prices are marked and firmly set (no haggling, except at the strawmarket). Almost every store takes at least three major credit cards (usually American Express, MasterCard, and Visa, but Diners Club and Carte Blanche are popular, too).

Some items are real buys in Nassau; others are not the bargains they may appear to be. That there is no sales tax is a saving in itself. Your best strategy is to make a shopping list ahead of time and check out a few prices in your local stores before making the trip. Then decide what you want to shop for here. U.S. citizens can take home $400 worth of duty-free merchandise per person.

Shopping hours are usually 9 or 9:30 A.M. to 5 P.M., six days a week. A few stores close one afternoon a week, however, so double-check if you have a particular goal in mind.

Many of the walkways are shaded so that the sun won't cramp your style. Put on your shorts, jeans, or other casual wear (absolutely no swimsuits downtown, please!) and begin strolling. Your starting point could be Rawson Square, where the cruise ships come in, right across from the government buildings. Most of the shopping area will be to your right (west), but make a quick left to visit what may be the island's best location for watches and cameras.

John Bull is on the near side of Bay Street, just a block east of your starting point, and it gets all the rave reviews in newspapers and magazines for Nassau's best prices. One entire room is devoted to Rolex, Seiko, Pulsar Quartz, and other watches. Corum and Les Musts de Cartier are in the main room, but a big selection of Canon cameras takes up almost as much space. You'll also find gold chains, other jewelry, and an entire office supplies shop in the back.

The **Perfume Bar** has several branches in Nassau, including one on Bank Lane. You should be aware that prices for perfume and cologne are fixed in Nassau, so there's no point in wandering through store after store in search of the best buy. Just make sure they have the brand you want.

Leather Masters, a little shop on Bank Lane, could be your next stop. Don't let the forest of Gucci handbags intimidate you; there are other very attractive purses here, too, plus a good selection of belts.

Fashionable resort wear isn't that easy to find in downtown Nassau, but you may find what you're looking for at **Cole's of Nassau,** 10 Parliament Street, particularly if your tastes run toward the prep styles. It looks and feels like a friendly small-town dress shop and carries a good selection of sundresses, shorts, nightgowns, lingerie, and shoes. When you've overdosed on Androsia batik, this is the place to come.

The English Shop, on the same block, has a nice antique-shop feel. Beautiful hand-crocheted and embroidered table-cloths are the attraction, and you'll also find English teas, honeys, and a few small antiques.

Colombian Emeralds, on Bay Street west of Parliament, virtually sparkles green with its elegant wares. There are unmounted stones for sale at $300–$3,000 per carat, and even a totally uneducated eye can peer into the display cases and see the difference. Just when you're asking yourself who would come here to buy unmounted emeralds, you notice photos on the wall of U.S. TV personalities who appear to be satisfied customers. There are beautiful pieces of emerald jewelry and watches, lighters, gold gift items, and jewelry made of other precious stones. If you'd rather pick up a gift of Waterford crystal or Royal Doulton china, walk through the inner doorway to **Treasure Trove** for a fine selection of both.

Pipe of Peace, nearby on Bay Street, sells a lot more than pipes these days. It's really a men's shop with a selection of watches (Seiko and Citizen), cameras (Nikon and Olympus), stereo components (Aiwa), Dunhill pipes and lighters, and elegant grooming and toiletry kits for travel. The glass antique cars inside glass bottles make nice gifts.

Solomon's Mines, next door, has the kind of gimmicky name some shoppers instinctively don't trust. But give it a chance; it was the first store in town to carry Giorgio cologne, and it has a big selection of Royal Doulton and other fine china, plus a small selection of Waterford crystal.

Bernard's, also on Bay Street, keeps its best stuff in the back room. There you'll find fabulous Lalique, a lovely selection of Baccarat crystal, and spectacular Baccarat candelabras starting at $500 or so. There's lots of Wedgwood up front.

Charlotte Street may be the best side street in Nassau for interesting buys, and **Coin of the Realm** is certainly one of its most interesting shops. An armed guard admits you to this small 200-year-old building, where you'll find coin jewelry, escudos, treasure coins, old bank notes, watches, all kinds of jewelry, and antique maps. Stamp collectors can leaf through the offerings (mostly Bahamian), which start at $5 or so, or choose one of the costlier examples ($300 and up) from the display cases. Serious collectors may be invited into the back room, where the rarities are priced from $3,000.

The two **Brass & Leather Shops** on Charlotte Street are filled with elegant merchandise. You might choose a Land briefcase, a Gucci bag, a silver flask, an elegant belt or scarf, or almost anything made of English brass or copper.

The Scottish Shop is an unusual and appealing two-floor store featuring a little of everything from—where else?—Scotland: character dolls from Clark and Vivien (dressed as Rhett and Scarlett) to Charles and Di (dressed for their wedding), Scottish shortbread, paperweights, and a list of last names, each matched to the appropriate tartan. The tartans themselves, with the sweaters and other clothing, are upstairs.

Balmain Antiques, a second-floor shop on the other side of Charlotte Street, is easy to miss. It feels a little more like an art gallery than a retail outlet, but you can find an attractive souvenir to take home and hang on a wall. Framed antique maps are $10–$1,700 and up, matted ship scenes are $50–$200 or so, and framed ship scenes (there are just a few) are $24–$36. You can buy artwork elsewhere and bring it here for custom framing.

The Nassau Shop at 284 Bay Street is the largest store in town and the closest you'll find to department store shopping. The biggest attraction is a huge ground-floor selection of men's sweaters and wool scarves, lots of them from Braemar, and a large selection of cosmetics, Samsonite luggage, and swim wear. Watches include Piaget, Baume & Mercier, and a number of less expensive brands. Closed Thursday afternoon.

The Island Shop, on the corner of Bay and Charlotte, is worth visiting primarily for the second-floor selection of books and magazines. They always seem to have the hot authors' latest, only weeks after the *New York Times* reviews appear—plus art, language, and guide books and lots of paperback fiction just right for beach and poolside reading.

The Heirloom and **The Porcelain Gallery** are two small sister shops on Frederick Street, both with thick carpets and a don't-touch atmosphere that can be a little off-putting. The former, where local brides register their china and silver patterns, has lovely selections from Germany. The latter, which carries Wilkens china and silver (also from Germany), could be the place where you'll find the perfect antique to remember this visit by: perhaps a rosewood lap desk, a framed print, a brooch, a pendant. Most of the merchandise is from England.

The Perfume Shop, at the corner of Bay and Frederick, is a pleasant little store with lots of fragrance testers (from Joy to Chanel No. 5). All prices are clearly marked in the display cases. Men's fragrances, too.

Old Nassau, also on Bay near Frederick, is a lot larger than its narrow facade would indicate. The front room is owned by John Bull, so you can find the same good prices on watches (Concorde, Seiko, Pulsar, Omega, Ebel, Raymond Weil, Les Musts de Cartier, Corum, Rolex). The same goes for cameras (Nikon, Canon, Olympus, Konika, Pentax, Hasselblad,

Mamiya). Pearls, charms, and other jewelry are available. The back rooms of the store, not connected with John Bull, include a shoe store, china and crystal shops, and a comprehensive hardware department where you can pick up an ice chest for a picnic.

City Pharmacy, nearby on Bay, is a real hometown drugstore with medicines, greeting cards (the old-fashioned kind), perfumes, and even board games like Monopoly. There's a big suntan lotion selection, and this is one of the few places you *might* find Bain de Soleil without crossing over to Paradise Island.

Carib Jewellers on Bay has a wide selection of Casio watches (and more expensive brands) and a nice selection of German crystal and china in the back. Those glass ships inside glass bottles (similar to the glass cars at Pipe of Peace) make nice gifts.

The open-air **Straw Market** at the corner of Bay and Market is a must for visitors who want to take home one of those colorful hand-decorated straw bags made here. You'll see similarly designed hats, dolls, and other creations, too. Be prepared to haggle over price and to pay cash.

Lightbourn's, on Bay between Market and George, is one of the most attractive perfume shops in town, offering a large selection of men's and women's fragrances and some pretty atomizers from England. All prices are clearly marked in the display cases.

When you reach the Sheraton at the end of Bay Street, go through the entrance to find a small shopping arcade. **Trader Vic's** is the best shop here, but it ought to change its name. While it has a few Hawaiian shirts, men's wool sweaters are the attraction. You might find a real hand-knit Irish fisherman's sweater for a better price than elsewhere in town. The sweaters bear British labels like Dalkeith, Lyle & Scott, and Braemar. And the shop is open on Sundays, which is unusual in Nassau.

It may look as though the shopping district ends here, but Nassau's two best women's boutiques are still to come. Walk about two blocks past the Sheraton to find **Ambrosine** at West Bay and Marlborough. Both local and U.S. customers come here to find fabulous silk (or very good polyester) dresses for special evenings, very fashionable swimsuits (including Ostermans from Israel), and a good selection of sundresses.

Impact, the next store down, is the place to go when you want to add a touch of the outrageous to your wardrobe. If you miss the colorful fashion designers back home, you'll be delighted to find the type here, perhaps selling a young customer on a new dress by remarking, "I love the way it makes you walk." There's lots of glitter, sparkle, and sexiness in these clothes (need a black leather swimsuit with hobnail trim?), and there are quieter garments, too.

If you're staying in one of the large hotels, you could do a lot of your shopping, for both gifts and necessities, right there. The Ambassador Beach has the best drugstore and the Cable Beach the biggest selection, overall, of shops.

Don't expect to do last-minute shopping at the Nassau airport. Other than a small selection of perfumes, the best you'll do there is a T-shirt and a bottle of booze.

Most Paradise Island hotel guests take the ferry across to Nassau for at least one Bay Street shopping expedition, yet they have their own smaller shopping center just down the street from the Britannia and within easy walking distance of Loews Harbour Cove.

The 11-store Paradise Shopping Center includes branches of John Bull, Mademoiselle, Colombian Emeralds, and Pipe of Peace. Francesca's is one of the nicest shops, with a good selection of sexy Vanity Fair lingerie and nightgowns. You'll also find a deli (the Village Gourmet), a pizza place (Swank Pizza), and a newsstand.

NIGHTLIFE

Nassau and Paradise Island take pride in the variety of their nightlife. While the emphasis is on the noisier activities, there are choices to suit every taste, and they range from the sounds of steel drums to the constant clatter of the slot machines. So pick a casino, go to a show, visit the local night spots, and get to know the Bahamians. Or just sail away under the moonlight with a tall, cold Goombay Smash in hand. You could try something new every night, or you might find a favorite spot and become a regular during your stay.

The casinos are Nassau's best-known night spots, and the **Paradise Island Casino** began it all. Thanks to a $1.5-million renovation in 1984 and an expansion in 1987, the 20,000-square-foot casino is more glamorous than ever with a mirrored ceiling, a $50,000 chandelier made of brass palm leaves, Doric columns, and a new coral, green, and white color scheme. The casino can provide both daytime and nighttime amusement: The blackjack and craps tables open at noon, and the slot machines (all 1,000 of them) are available 24 hours a day. At night the casino goes into full action, adding tables for roulette, Big Six, and baccarat.

And at night, it's on with the show. You can see Paradise Island's 90-minute casino production as a dinner show or later in the evening with only drinks served. If you're staying at the Paradise Island Resort on its Gourmet Dining Plan, the show is free.

Be prepared for glitter, because that's what these shows are about. A recent one opened with a bare-breasted blonde in a tiara, glittered bikini, and ostrich plumes, descending in a gilded cage. The evening's first magic trick was turning a dog into a scantily clad dancing girl. And later we saw a live tiger, panther, and (caged) lion on stage. The costumes were spectacular, the British comedian likeable, some of the acrobatic dancing very impressive, and there was clever use of film, with live performers appearing to walk in and out of the on-screen action.

The casino is located between the Grand Britannia and Paradise Towers hotels and can be reached by walking indoors through either of the lobbies. For show reservations, call 326–3000. In the U.S., call (800) 321–3000.

The **Cable Beach Casino,** located at Nassau's hotel of the same name, is a relative newcomer to the gambling scene, and the developers knew exactly who they were competing with when they designed it. It was created to match the original Paradise Island facility, point for point.

Its 20,000 square feet contain 44 blackjack tables, six for craps, four for roulette, one for baccarat, and 526 slot machines. The 300 croupiers are all women. And if you're truly a small-time gambler, you could be happy here: there are nickel slot machines.

Its casino shows have been winning rave reviews, too. A recent one had the good taste to use Gershwin music to set a certain mood for its incredibly expensive sets and leggy showgirls. Shows at 9 and 11 P.M. Tuesday through Sunday. For reservations or information, call 327–6200. Tickets were recently priced at $28, $22, and $15.

To reach the casino, walk through the Cable Beach Hotel lobby and past its indoor shopping arcade.

DANCE THE NIGHT AWAY

If you're looking for the most fashionable and glamorous disco in town, you'll find it at the Sheraton Grand Hotel on Paradise Island. **Le Paon** (the peacock) has been the island's "in" spot for several years now, a title it could have won on looks alone. It's located at the back of the Grand's lobby, behind double glass doors. There are green plants in gleaming brass tubs, an entryway floor of red bricks laid out in concentric circles, two huge round mirrors in back with stylized peacock heads etched in white, a handsome bar to the right, tiny glittery golden lights, and a sunken dance floor. Banquettes and tables furnish the main room. If you have a touch of romance in your soul, head straight for the back room with its gorgeous picture-window view of the beach.

Happy hour at Le Paon is 5–9 P.M. After nine, dress up a little to enjoy the lively hours ahead.

On the other hand, should you ask Nassau residents to name their favorite spot for late-night dancing, they'd probably name the **Palace Disco** on Elizabeth Avenue, just off Bay Street. It draws a mixed crowd of Bahamians and tourists and goes strong Tuesdays through Saturdays from 9 P.M. until 4 A.M.

The decor is disco-modern, with vertical mirror strips at the entrance, brown and chrome chairs at wooden tables, and a railing separating the smallish, round dance floor from the horseshoe-shaped bar and the rest of the room. An upstairs balcony has a bar, mostly with tables for two overlooking the action. Both disco and live music are part of the scene every night. Telephone 325–7733.

Ronnie's Rebel Room is the place to go when you're in the mood for all those island attractions you went on vacation to see. You'll find a limbo dancer, a fire dancer, a steel drummer, and Calypso revival singers here, just outside the Nassau shopping district. But plan ahead; there are shows only three nights a week: Wednesday and Saturday at 8 and 10:15 P.M., Tuesday at 10:15.

It's on West Bay Street, next to the Atlantis Hotel. Telephone 323–4483. Reservations recommended.

The Grand Hotel also features a typically Bahamian show, **The Junkanoo Revue,** on Wednesday night. Sabu the Great, an authentically costumed voodoo dancer, stars in this panoply of glass eating, fire dancing, limboing, and steel band music. Come for a barbecue dinner at 7 P.M. or for the show alone at 8:15. Telephone 326–2011, extension 667.

Other nightlife possibilities include **Peanuts Taylor's Drumbeat Club** and its nightly Afro-Bahamian Revue (West Bay Street, telephone 322–4233) and live music at **The Back Room** disco (Balmoral Beach Hotel, Cable Beach, telephone 327–7481).

MOONLIGHT CRUISES

If your idea of a perfect evening is something quieter, why not choose a romantic moonlight cruise? The **Nautilus Dinner Cruise** takes you out on the 97-foot glass-bottom boat at 7 P.M. any evening, Monday through Saturday. Thanks to the powerful underwater lights, you'll be able to see all the colorful marine life as you float along. This tour leaves from the New Mermaid Marina at the corner of Bay and Deveaux streets, next to Captain Nemo's restaurant. Telephone 325–2871 for reservations and current prices. Or make arrangements through your hotel's tour desk.

Perhaps even more romantic is the **Wild Harp Sunset Dinner Cruise** aboard an elegant 56-foot sailing schooner. You'll leave at 6 P.M. from the Nassau Yacht Haven (or at 6:15 from Loew's Harbour Cove Hotel, if you're staying on Paradise Island), then sail into the sunset with the lights of Nassau Harbour and its huge cruise ships as your backdrop. The tour includes the three-hour cruise, a buffet dinner under the stars, a welcoming cocktail, one complimentary glass of wine with dinner, and live music. There's a cash bar for any additional drinks you want to order. Telephone 322–1149 (daytime) or 324–1206 (at night), or make reservations at your hotel's tour desk.

Local tour companies also offer a variety of night club, cabaret/casino, and pub-crawling tours. For Tropical Travel Tours (Gray Line), telephone 322–4091; for Curtis Brothers Travel & Tour Company, telephone 323–5977.

FREEPORT/LUCAYA

Tourism seems well developed here, and it was planned that way. In 1964 there were eight hotel rooms on Grand Bahama Island; today there are more than 3,500, and its capital, Free-port/Lucaya, is the Bahamas' second largest city.

Chances are you'll arrive at the Freeport airport and taxi to the Princess or Princess Tower hotels, which are across the street from one another. Until you're ready to go to the beach, everything you'll want to see is right here: the casino, the International Bazaar, and the restaurants—all owned by Princess International.

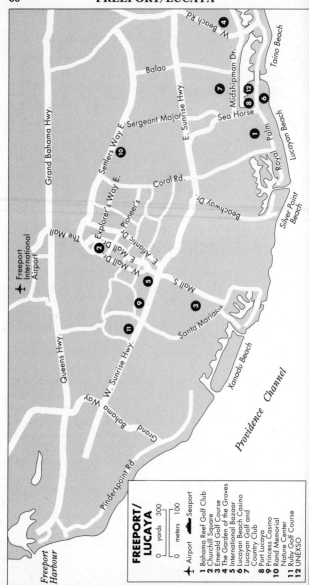

FREEPORT/
LUCAYA

✈ Airport ⚓ Seaport

0 yards 300
0 meters 100

1 Bahama Reef Golf Club
2 Churchill Square
3 Emerald Golf Course
4 The Garden of the Groves
5 International Bazaar
6 Lucayan Beach Casino
7 Lucayan Golf and
   Country Club
8 Port Lucaya
9 Princess Casino
10 Rand Memorial
   Nature Center
11 Ruby Golf Course
12 UNEXSO

The **Princess Country Club** is the garden property, with its manicured lawns separated from the sister hotel by a four-lane street and a pedestrian walkway. This low, rambling building, the older of the two, has undergone refurbishing in recent years. The rather formal royal blue and ivory lobby remains, but almost everything else has been changed.

The pool area is something special, with waterfalls and a Jacuzzi set among artificial rock formations. The open-air poolside restaurant, John B., has been redone with thatched roof, ceiling fans, and lots of greenery.

The Princess's rooms ($85–$140, single or double) were set up motel style, and the decor will depend on which wing you end up in. Ask for something in the renovated 700 Wing, and you'll find two double beds with rattan headboards and peach print spreads, matching draperies, beige carpet, a closet with sliding mirrored doors, a wallpapered bath with a marble vanity, cable TV, and direct-dial touch-tone phone.

The 900 Wing was built as the deluxe area; it has larger rooms and separate dressing areas outside the baths.

Guanahani's is the glamour restaurant at the Princess. It's a separate little house with a glass wall overlooking the pool (so you can watch the last sunbathers), bleached wood walls, rattan chairs with dark green or soft coral batik cushions, lots of lush potted plants, brass ceiling fans, and huge chandeliers. Dinner includes salad, bread, vegetables, and dessert as well as Bahamian-style main courses like orange marmalade chicken and papaya ginger pork.

One new Country Club benefit is a complete fitness center offering massages, facials, saunas, exercise equipment, and a variety of dance classes. The hotel also boasts a golf shop, the Patio restaurant for American and Bahamian cuisine, and The Rib Room, known for great steaks.

The 10-story **Princess Tower,** built in 1970, attracts the high-rollers, conference groups, and an urban East Coast crowd. Expect to find the little luxuries as well as cable TV, telephones, and air-conditioning. The ninth and tenth floors have been turned into a "towers" section, with concierge, private check-in, a breakfast room, and other extras.

The service is unusually gracious. As at its sister property, room rates range from $85 to $140, single or double.

Princess Country Club, Box F-2623, Freeport, Grand Bahama. (809) 352–6721. Princess Tower, (809) 352–9661 or (800) 223–1818.

The **Casino,** next door, was completely refurbished in 1986. You'll find a handsome new circular bar overlooking the action, the rather formal Crown Room gourmet buffet restaurant, the casual Garden Cafe (open till 4 A.M. for hungry gamblers), and a $100,000 jackpot. Amusements include blackjack, roulette, and slot machines.

The glittery casino show manages to charm almost everybody at one point or another. Nightly at 8:30 and 10:45. Your ticket includes two drinks and gratuities. Telephone (809) 352–7811.

Xanadu Beach & Marina Resort, Freeport's only major beachside hotel, reopened in 1985 with a variety of accommodations. Guests can choose from rooms in the 12-story tower, the pool wing, or the two-story villas. Rooms are $150; villas, accommodating up to six people, are $375–$650.

Tennis, on-site water sports, pool, sauna, and a marina await you. Restaurants include the Persian Room for Continental cuisine, the Escoffier Room for French specialties, and the Tiffany Room for American and Bahamian dishes. For nightlife, there's dancing to live music at Port of Call or a more intimate evening at Xanadu Lounge, the hotel's piano bar. And the management likes to point out that the casino isn't far away.

Xanadu Beach and Marina Resort, Box F-2438, Freeport, Grand Bahama. (800) 222–3788 or (809) 352–8720.

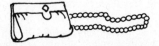

Once you've won all that money at the casino, you'll want to spend it at the 10-acre **International Bazaar.** Enter through the red-lacquer Japanese gate several yards down the way, or just keep walking past the Princess Tower and the casino, then slip into the first pavilion. The dozens of stores represent 25 countries, and every visitor should schedule at least half a day to stroll through them, even if only to window shop. If the settings look as though they're straight out of the movies, it's because the entire bazaar was designed by a Hollywood special effects man and built in 1967 at a cost of $4 million.

The stores all accept major credit cards. You'll find a map posted at the entrance; in alphabetical order, here are some shops to check out.

Androsia of Lucaya is just that, a big selection of Androsia batik fashions, made in the Bahamas. Garments include sundresses, bikinis, tube tops, skirts, and culottes.

Bahama Coin & Stamp Ltd. is a tiny shop worth looking into, whether you're a collector or an amateur looking for an unusual souvenir. On the cheap side, there are coin sets for as little as $5, uncirculated Bahamian three-dollar bills for $5.95, and a set of four Churchill stamps for $5. The more elegant items include the Krugerrand money clip ($1,175) and the Bahamian $100 gold piece ($650). There are Roman coins from A.D. 350–530 too.

Colombian Emeralds is a bigger, friendlier store than its branch in Nassau. Unmounted emeralds, amethysts and other stones are in a separate room. A variety of merchandise, including coral jewelry, pearls, and watches, are in the main room.

Gemini I, where rock music always plays in the background, is a boutique for the young and modern, featuring shoes, belts, casual jewelry, and all kinds of accessories. Look for the great collection of evening bags in a variety of fabrics and styles.

Ginza appears to be the place to buy a watch, thanks to what may be the lowest prices in town on Seiko, Citizen, Pulsar Quartz, Rolex, Les Musts de Cartier, Piaget, and more. A good selection of cameras, a separate room of Mikimoto pearls and other jewelry, plus a friendly, helpful sales staff make this store an inviting shopping experience.

The **Island Galleria** used to be an art gallery, and there are still watercolors and prints for sale in the back (most in the $100–$500 range). Up front, it's now a very classy, spacious store with a good selection of jewelry, watches, china, and Waterford crystal.

Leather & Things has briefcases, picture frames, backgammon sets, purses, luggage, desk sets, and even elegant tool kits in leather. A handsome store, although the bargains may not be enormous; a briefcase that was $129 in Nassau was only $5 less here.

The **London Pacesetter Boutique** is a small corner shop with large possibilities. Merchandise includes fashionable Gottex swimsuits, trendy resort wear, and a selection of name-brand English sweaters.

Midnight Sun has two stores, both with lovely merchandise from Scandinavia and elsewhere. The first is the most formal, with frosted Finnish glass, Lalique figurines, and Baccarat glassware. The second, catty-corner from the first, carries everything from Johnson Brothers ironstone to brightly colored hair combs from Copenhagen.

The attractive and tasteful **Old Curiosity Shop** specializes in antique and reproduction jewelry. Brass, copperware, silverplate, and clocks sell well, too. Most of the things are from England, and some have come from France, Germany, or Holland.

Scandia Solomon's Mines is worth a visit for the selection of Waterford crystal.

Tivoli, a very chic little Scandinavian store, offers ordinary items made special by Danish design: housewares, games, jewelry, clothing, candles.

There's a strawmarket at the far end of the International Bazaar, where you can buy locally made bags, hats, and the like. Walk by fast if you're not interested; the sales pitch can be presented insistently.

There are any number of places to stop for a meal during your shopping spree. Among the most interesting are the following international spots.

The **Japanese Steak House and Tea Garden,** next to Ginza, serves an outdoor lunch 11:30–3:30 and dinner 5:30–10:30 P.M. A large green Buddha welcomes you at the top of the stairs. Eating outdoors provides the most fun; although you'll sit at very un-Japanese orange plastic chairs, you can look down on Asia to your left and on the boulevards of France to your right.

Michel's, a sidewalk cafe on Place des Wallons, serves both lunch and dinner underneath blue and white umbrellas, on wine-label-design tablecloths. Dinner entrees, served 5–11 P.M., include red snapper *beurre noisette* and *entrecôte café de Paris.* During the day, have something more casual: deep-fried shrimp or half a papaya filled with chicken salad.

Rendezvous, another outdoor cafe, is just down the boulevard in "France." You can get sandwiches, burgers, and light lunch platters during the day and more substantial fare at night. The setting is very Parisian, with red, white, and blue umbrellas and lacy white wrought-iron chairs.

The **Sir Winston Churchill Pub** is at the very end of the bazaar, across the street from the straw market. This is a true meeting place at any time of day (open 11 A.M.–4 A.M.), perfect if you want to make new friends in Freeport. You can eat in the garden or in the cozy publike dining room. Choices range from fish and chips to six kinds of pizza, from cracked conch to broiled lobster.

The pub itself is quite large, with banquettes and chairs in that dark, faded green you've seen in libraries and university clubs. Houndstooth wallpaper, ceiling fans, pawn-shop-globe light fixtures, and photos of both Churchill and the queen complete the authentic British mood. Because the jukebox plays loud rock in mid-afternoon, the nights with live music are the best meeting times.

For another helping of British food, go to **Pub on the Mall** the next day. Open for both lunch and dinner (till 4 A.M.), this stone and cross-timber building across the street from the International Bazaar is a popular late-night gathering place. Menu choices include steak and kidney pie, Welsh rarebit, and fish and chips.

When you want a special dinner outside the hotel complex, **Ruby Swiss** is the place to go. Near the golf course and just a short taxi ride from the Princess Hotels, this unimposing restaurant in a former private home is considered Freeport's best by many people. The setting is more casual than the ads indicate, with red napkins, blue tablecloths, beamed ceilings, tall windows, and live music every night. There's even a tiny dance floor.

The Ruby Swiss menu is extensive. Swiss specialties include *zuercher geschnetzeltes* (veal in wine sauce with *roesti*), *schafhauser sauerbraten* (a braised beef with red cabbage), *Engadiner goulash, wiener schnitzel, fondue bourguignon,* and seafood choices from conch to lobster thermidor.

The crowd is mostly couples with a well-scrubbed middle-America look (men in short-sleeve knit shirts, women in casual skirts and blouses). Best time to go: sunset. The blue-gray sky against tall pines afterward makes a perfect dinnertime view. Telephone 352–8507.

Pier I is for the night you want true seaside atmosphere. This little wooden house is built on stilts right in the water of Freeport Harbour. The mood is casual, with a fabulous sea view and refreshing ocean breeze. Seafood is the specialty. Telephone 352–6674.

To get there, take West Sunrise Highway through the industrial section. When the road ends, make a left and follow the Freeport Harbour signs. At the green and white restaurant sign, turn right. Don't worry about getting home: This is where cruise ships come in, and a line of taxis is usually waiting.

The **Captain's Charthouse Restaurant** is the place for steak, but don't expect a romantic view—it's right on the highway. Just take West Sunrise until you see the restaurant sign and the two-story brown wooden building on your right. Now open for both lunch and dinner, with special prices that start at $6.95 if you eat early (5–6:30 P.M.). Other specialties include lobster, prime rib, and live Calypso dinner music. Telephone 373–3900.

The **Stoned Crab** could be a beach house that belongs to a well-to-do friend. It seems to be nothing but pointed thatched roofs and glass, with a huge fig tree out front and the beach out back. Eat indoors on small wooden tables and captain's chairs, with a view of palm trees and beach, or take a table on the patio out back. You're on the beach. You'll find American and Bahamian specialties on the menu. Telephone 373–1442.

To get there, take East Sunrise to Sea Horse Road to Midshipman Road. Turn right at the old stone sign that has letters missing and now says "rtun marind." You'll cross a little bridge and see the restaurant signs.

This is the beach at Lucaya, and here you'll discover how the other half lives on Grand Bahama Island. While the gamblers and the sophisticates haunt Freeport, Lucaya draws a younger, more active, more casual crowd (including beach bums and divers) taking advantage of inexpensive vacation packages.

The **Holiday Inn** is one of the area's top gathering places. Its lower-level disco and nightclub, Panache, draws both singles and couples. If there's a place to make new friends, it's here among the salmon-pink leather banquettes and rattan chairs. The cover charge includes two drinks. Open 9 P.M.–3 A.M. Telephone 373–1333.

The hotel itself is a modern white structure right on the beach. The low-lighted, marble-floored lobby has intimate conversation groupings of blue print sofas and is surrounded by shops, including a branch of Mademoiselle and a liquor store. The lower-level exercise center isn't huge, but it has a mirrored wall and gym equipment. Regular exercise classes are held here. The Troubador Room serves Continental and Bahamian cuisine by candlelight. Other features include pool, tennis, golf nearby, and all water sports.

There are three types of rooms ($96–$135 double). The beachfronts have a king-size bed, carpet, color TV, and a balcony. If you want a walk-in closet, ask for one of the corner beachfront rooms. The deluxe rooms have two double beds, a balcony, and a view of the pool. Superior rooms, which really are the hotel's standard offering, may overlook the garden or the roof of the hotel. If the view matters to you, ask first.

Holiday Inn/Lucaya Beach, Box F-2468, Freeport, Grand Bahama. (809) 373–1333.

The **Atlantik Beach Hotel,** the Holiday Inn's nextdoor neighbor, gained a refurbished lobby, library, and shopping arcade in its most recent renovation.

Room rates are $110–$115 double, $105–$160 for suites, and a concierge floor, the Corona Classic Club, has been added.

Hotel guests have access to tennis courts, a large rectangular pool, an excellent beach, and windsurfing.

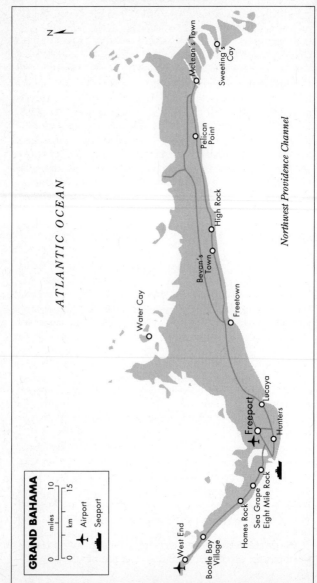

GRAND BAHAMA

ATLANTIC OCEAN

Northwest Providence Channel

McLean's Town

Sweeting's Cay

Pelican Point

High Rock

Bevan's Town

Freetown

Water Cay

Lucaya

Freeport

Hunters

Sea Grape

Eight Mile Rock

Homes Rock

Bootle Bay Village

West End

miles   10
km   15

✈ Airport

⚓ Seaport

Atlantik Beach Hotel, Box F-531, Freeport, Grand Bahama, or Airport Executive Tower #1, 1150 N.W. 72d Avenue, Miami, FL 33126. (809) 373-1444, (800) 622-6770, or (305) 592-5757.

The **Lucayan Beach Resort & Casino** opened its doors in 1986. The oceanside main hotel went into operation, complete with casino, restaurants, bars, pool, theater, cabaret, and almost 250 guest rooms ($120–$175, single or double). Dining choices include French food at Les Oursins, international buffets in the Lucayan Room, and casual American and island specialties at Hemingways. The resort's on-premise activities include deep-sea fishing, windsurfing, sailing, tennis, glass-bottom boat tours, and scuba diving. UNEXSO (Underwater Explorers Society) is here, offering a variety of complete diving vacations.

Lucayan Beach Resort & Casinos, Box F-336, Lucaya, Grand Bahama. (809) 373-7777 or (800) 772-1227.

The island of Grand Bahama is almost 100 miles long, and the West End district is a good 25 miles from the casino and bazaar. Here you'll find **Jack Tar Village,** a 2,000-acre resort run very much like Club Med. Pay $160 single or $240 double per day, then relax: Everything is included. That means all meals, unlimited liquor (even Club Med doesn't offer that), unlimited wine with meals, tennis, golf, water sports, entertainment, and all other activities. A saltwater pool, a beach, marina, shopping arcade, and disco await you. The only thing you'll have to pay extra for is your golf cart. Even a midnight snack is part of the package.

Jack Tar Village, 403 South Ackard, Dallas, TX 75202. (800) 527-9299 or (809) 346-6211.

The other reason most visitors to Grand Bahama drive west is to visit the **Buccaneer Club** for drinks, dinner, and the seaside atmosphere. The best way to go may be to take a tour. Local tour operators offer a Buccaneer Club beach party at least twice a week. The $27 price includes an open bar (for one hour), appetizers, dinner, transportation, and tips.

Harry's American Bar, another popular but out-of-the-way spot for drinks and dinner, is right down the way.

The large, well-known resorts aren't your only accommodation choices on Grand Bahama. A number of smaller hotels, most with air-conditioned rooms and all with at least one swimming pool, offer a variety of vacation experiences. All rates listed are per room, double occupancy, for the winter season. Reservations can be made directly with each hotel or through the **Bahamas Reservation Service,** (800) 327–0787.

Castaways Resort, 136 rooms and 1 suite, near the International Bazaar and Princess Casino, $60, (809) 352–6682.

Channel House Resort Club, 19 apartments, each with full kitchen, in Lucaya, about 150 yards from the beach, $72–$84, (809) 373–5405.

Coral Beach Hotel, a 10-unit apartment hotel right on the beach, $65–$79, (809) 373–2468.

Freeport Inn, 170 rooms, many with kitchenettes, near both the bazaar and the casino, $49–$69, (809) 352–6648.

New Victoria Inn, 40 rooms, scuba diving instruction available, $64, (809) 373–3040.

Silver Sands, 144 studios and 20 one-bedroom suites, less than 100 yards from the beach, $75–$105, (809) 373–5700.

Windward Hotel, 100 rooms (including some suites), near the bazaar and casino, $78, (809) 352–8221.

Organized tours can be the best way to enjoy the watery side of Grand Bahama, particularly if you're staying in downtown Freeport, and they're the best way to see the sights. Choices include a city bus tour that visits Garden of the Groves (a 12-acre botanical garden), the sunset booze cruise or wine-&-cheese cruise, a deep-sea fishing trip, trimaran sailing, glass-bottom boat trips, and scuba diving tours. One of the newest activities is a swim *with* Atlantic bottleneck dolphins trained by UNEXSO ($45). Tour prices range from $10 to $60 per person. Check with your hotel for further information.

Getting to Freeport/Lucaya is the easiest part of your vacation. Several major airlines fly here from U.S. cities, and Bahamasair has frequent service from Nassau.

Unless you plan a lot of exploring, your own two feet and an occasional taxi are all the local transportation you'll need. If you want to rent a car and see Grand Bahama on your own, Avis, Budget, Dollar, and National are among the rental companies at the Freeport airport.

ELEUTHERA AND
HARBOUR ISLAND

The sand really *is* pink in Harbour Island, but you have to take a close look to tell. When you do, you'll see tiny grains of pink coral sparkling in the sun.

Technically, Harbour Island isn't even part of Eleuthera. Yet this two-square-mile island off the larger island's northern coast has become the center of Eleutheran tourism.

After your flight to North Eleuthera, take a taxi to the ferry. At the end of this short journey you'll find yourself in 300-year-old Dunmore Town, just minutes from your hotel: Several choices are lined up on the northern beach.

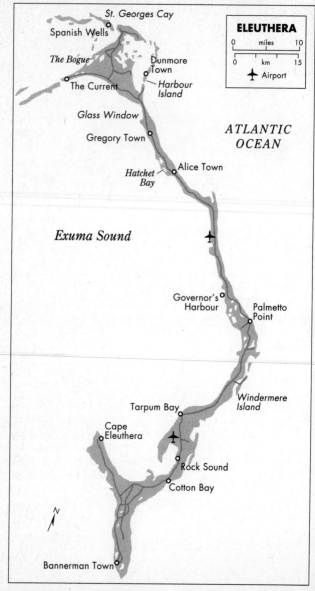

St. Georges Cay

Spanish Wells

The Bogue

Dunmore
Town

The Current
*Harbour
Island*

ELEUTHERA

| 0 | miles | 10 |
| 0 | km | 15 |

✈ Airport

Glass Window

Gregory Town

*ATLANTIC
OCEAN*

Alice Town

*Hatchet
Bay*

Exuma Sound

Governor's
Harbour

Palmetto
Point

*Windermere
Island*

Tarpum Bay

Cape
Eleuthera

Rock Sound

Cotton Bay

N

Bannerman Town

Pink Sands was established a long time ago, when the wealthy still vacationed by going away to "camp," which meant resorts of rustic stone cabins with forestlike grounds, lots of privacy, and lots of cachet. Many of today's guests (average age 45-plus) have been coming since then.

Pink Sands is a little old-fashioned, and that's the essence of its charm. Men wear coats and ties to dinner. The dinner music is a nonamplified Calypso band. And the staff will still come to your cottage and prepare breakfast in your own kitchen. The cottages ($110–$153, Full American Plan) have ceiling fans and sliding glass doors leading onto the patio. There's no air-conditioning, but the ocean breezes feel wonderful. Tennis and water sports are available.

Pink Sands, Box 87, Harbour Island, Bahamas. (809) 333–2030.

The **Coral Sands Hotel,** just down the beach, is a much more informal, action-oriented resort. There are 33 rooms ($115 double), air-conditioned during the summer, tennis, water sports, and a dining room with Bahamian cuisine. Closed September through mid-November.

Coral Sands Hotel, Harbour Island, Bahamas. (809) 333–2350.

At the **Dunmore Beach Club** the same people come back year after year, often making reservations at check-out time. You can see the resort's hillside white gazebo from the beach. A closer look reveals the hotel's charm: lots of white wicker, greenery, and yellow accents, one-and two-bedroom cottage units with patios, and what even the competition admits is the best food on Harbour Island.

Six cottage buildings accommodate 28 guests ($190 double, Full American Plan). It's usually closed May through August.

Dunmore Beach Club, Box 122, Harbour Island, Bahamas. (809) 333–2200.

The **Ocean View Club** has only eight rooms (every one different), a youngish clientele, and a lobby that seems like a cheerful living room, with its piano, fireplace, plank ceilings, and small alcove bar. Every room ($95 double) has an ocean view.

Ocean View Club, Box 134, Harbour Island, Bahamas. (809) 333–2276.

Romora Bay Club, on the eastern end of the island, has the loveliest grounds of any Harbour Island resort. Terraced gardens lead from the main building to the waterfront and bayside bar.

The main house lobby is very attractive with its fireplace, almost formal blue and white furniture, baby grand piano, and black-and-white checkerboard tile floor. Whether you stay here or elsewhere, it's a lovely place for dinner. Ask to sit in the front room, with its white, country-European feeling.

Rooms ($115–$165, Modified American Plan) are in air-conditioned villas. There's a strong emphasis on water sports here, including sailing trips, boat rentals, and complete scuba diving package vacations.

Romora Bay Club, Box 146, Harbour Island, Bahamas. (809) 333–2325 or (800) 327–8286.

Valentine's Yacht Club & Inn is downtown and anything but secluded. Many of the guests at this friendly hotel are divers (its own dive center is across the street); many others are the owners of boats docked at its 33-slip marina. Valentine's newest attraction is its harbor-front bar, The Reach.

The motel-style rooms ($90–$100 double, Modified American Plan) have queen-size beds, carpeting, and sliding glass doors. There's no room service, but they say a neighbor (known as Friendly Willy) will give you fresh fruit from his yard for a dollar if you walk outside your room and call his name.

The pool and hot tub are just outside the main building. This side of the island is beachless, but Valentine's has its own Dunes Club on the northern shore.

Valentine's Yacht Club, Box 1, Harbour Island, Bahamas. (809) 333–2142, (809) 333–2080, or (305) 491–1010.

Telephone service to Eleuthera is not always the best; you may want to write for reservations.

The hotels have strict meal hours, but you can eat at almost any time of day (well, until 9 P.M. or so; Harbour Island closes early) at **Angela's Starfish Restaurant** downtown. Enter the aqua stucco house, make your choices from the lengthy Bahamian menu (emphasis on seafood, of course), place your order at the window, then choose one of the small white tables or picnic tables outdoors. A delicious home-cooked meal will soon be placed before you. Telephone (809) 333–2253.

George's, the island's late-night spot of choice, looks a little like a private home turned roadside diner. It welcomes a crowd that's usually half tourists and half locals for live music and general hanging-out until 2 A.M. or so. For special events, there's a cover charge. This is the kind of place in which the noise level during a swimsuit fashion show rivals that at the average rock concert. To find George's, take the first right (going toward town) after Valentine's. Two more rights, and you're there.

Vic-Hum's (pronounced wick-ums, Bahamian style) is the island's other late-night choice, where you'll find fewer tourists.

Many visitors take day trips, by private boat or the local ferry, to Spanish Wells, a sparkling clean little fishing community that looks even more authentically New England than Harbour Island. Bonus: There are lots of straw goods here that make great gifts and souvenirs.

Seeing the rest of Eleuthera while staying in Harbour Island is not quite as easy. This island is so long and narrow that it has three airports.

One airport is in Governor's Harbour halfway down the coast, a town now dominated by a very active 53-acre **Club**

Med. This club's specialty is scuba diving, with daily expeditions (including one to the Exuma Wall) for experienced divers, and a series of four lessons leading to club certification for beginners. A complete photo lab is available for developing underwater pictures.

Other activities and special features include eight tennis courts, yoga, snorkeling, sailing, water-skiing, miniclubs (for parents who want to bring their kids without having to see them during the day), and a circus workshop in which guests of all ages can learn Big Top skills from juggling to the trapeze.

In the Club Med tradition, one-week vacations ($600–$1,150 plus airfare) include three meals a day, wine with lunch and dinner, and all activities. Lower prices are for stays in January or the first week of February; highest prices apply during the Christmas season. Telephone (800) 528–3100.

The **Cotton Bay Resort,** with 77 recently refurbished air-conditioned rooms ($300–$350, Modified American Plan) and an 18-hole golf course, has an equally elegant atmosphere and a similar clientele. Tennis, water sports, a private beach, beautiful new landscaping, and pink cottages that open right onto the beach are among the attractions. Box 28, Rock Sound, Eleuthera, Bahamas. (809) 334–2101.

The **Windermere Island Club,** 18 miles from the Rock Sound airport and set on a private island, can be described as understated, luxurious, and just a trifle snobbish. If you can get a reservation, you'll find 22 air-conditioned villas, rooms, and apartments ($330 double and up, Full American Plan), a private beach, pool, water sports, six tennis courts, and international cuisine. Like all the Rock Sound resorts, this one tends to be more formal during the winter season. Box 25, Rock Sound, Eleuthera, Bahamas. (809) 332–2538.

While Eleuthera has never officially been named the Bahamas' most beautiful island, many visitors are ready to give it their vote. Lush green foliage, resorts practically draped in bougainvillea, and 17th-century architecture add up to a very visual travel experience. If possible, try to see some of its natural glories on your own.

A long taxi trip up and down this 110-mile-long island

(only five miles wide at its widest point) could blow the budget, but there are several local car rental companies in Palmetto Point (next to Governor's Harbour), Rock Sound, and Harbour Island itself.

Sights to go out of your way for include the Glass Window (a spot near Upper Bogue where the island becomes so narrow that you're driving with the Atlantic on one side of the road and the bay on the other) and the pineapple plantation in Gregory Town.

The simplest and most pleasant solution may be an organized tour. A six-hour day trip run by Eleuthera Tours in Tarpum Bay includes most of the important sights. Other tour possibilities include snorkeling cruises, booze or wine-and-cheese cruises, moonlight beach parties, and island hops to Spanish Wells, Nassau, or Freeport.

Bahamasair has daily flights to the three Eleuthera airports, and there are direct flights from Miami to all three.

THE ABACOS

Not everyone in Colonial America was happy about the Declaration of Independence; some citizens were so upset that they sailed for the Abacos in the 1780s. English settlers were already there, and the descendants of both groups give this 130-mile-long island chain a true New England flavor. The Abacos may be among the most tourist-developed of the Out Islands, but few have accused it of being spoiled by progress.

TREASURE CAY

The largest and most formal resort in the Abacos is the **Treasure Cay Beach Hotel & Villas.** You can arrive by boat, as many visitors do, or fly to Treasure Cay. A short taxi ride over a bumpy dirt road brings you to the hotel's front door.

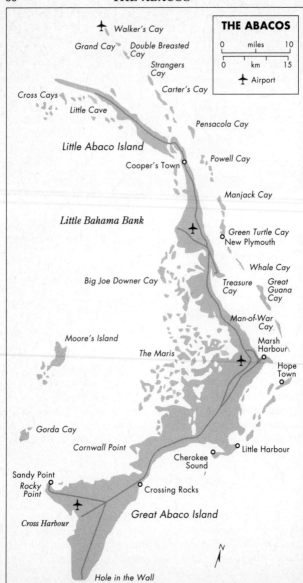

THE ABACOS

miles
0 10

km
0 15

✈ Airport

✈ Walker's Cay

Grand Cay   Double Breasted
            Cay

            Strangers
            Cay

            Carter's Cay

Cross Cays

Little Cave

            Pensacola Cay

Little Abaco Island

            Powell Cay

Cooper's Town

            Manjack Cay

Little Bahama Bank

            Green Turtle Cay
            New Plymouth

            Whale Cay

Big Joe Downer Cay   Treasure   Great
                         Cay   Guana
                                     Cay

                         Man-of-War
                         Cay

Moore's Island   Marsh
                        Harbour

            The Maris   Hope
                            Town

Gorda Cay

Cornwall Point   Little Harbour

                    Cherokee
                    Sound

Sandy Point
Rocky   Crossing Rocks
Point

Cross Harbour   Great Abaco Island

                    N

Hole in the Wall

There are luxuries here in the more than 200 hotel rooms, cottages, and villas that you won't find in other Out Island hotels. Even the standard rooms ($155 per person double, Full American Plan) in the main building are large, with two double beds, sand-colored carpet, garden view, satellite TV, and a dressing room with open closet. There are no telephones (you can wait your turn for the one in the lobby), and the bathrooms provide the world's smallest towels.

The fir-and-stucco duplex Harbour House accommodations are the resort's finest. You can rent a single bedroom, a one-bedroom suite, or various combinations thereof. The suite includes a small kitchen, a living room with sliding glass doors and marina view, and very private loft bedroom with adjoining bath. Rates for suites begin at $180 per person.

If you prefer cottage-style comfort, you have a choice of two-bedroom ocean-view apartments, two-bedroom villas, or one-bedroom villas (from $200 per person). The one-bedrooms are the most attractive, with floral print sofas and open kitchens with bars.

The marina may be Treasure Cay's main attraction, but the secluded beach alone is worth the trip. Spectacular at first sight, it has white sand so soft and fine it feels a little like powder between your toes. The light aqua water is as calm and clear as a pool.

Treasure Cay is one of those self-contained resorts you never have to leave. You have an 18-hole golf course, 10 tennis courts, five swimming pools, sailing, snorkeling, scuba diving, water-skiing, bikes for rent, and fishing boats for charter. The gift shop has all the china, crystal, and perfume you might have looked for in Nassau. The resort shopping center includes a liquor store, a beauty salon, a supermarket, and a post office.

Meals are taken at the harbor-view Spinnaker restaurant or the slightly more formal Abaco Room. This is one of the few Out Islands resorts where men wear jackets for dinner.

The Treasure Cay crowd is as polished as the resort: men with well-kept beards and good haircuts, women with salon-highlighted hair and perfectly even tans. This is the kind of place where you might hear a 20ish blonde insisting on immediate checkout because she's made up with her husband of three weeks—and her parents' plane is waiting to whisk her back to him.

Treasure Cay Services, 2801 Ponce de Leon Blvd., Coral Gables, FL 33134. (305) 525–7711, (809) 367–2847, or (800) 327–1584.

GREEN TURTLE CAY

For a more casual mood, consider the **Green Turtle Club** on nearby Green Turtle Cay. Taxi from airport to ferry and zip over to the hotel dock, where the debonair British manager Martin Havill often meets the boat personally.

Your first glimpse will take in the green canopy and some very relaxed people having drinks on the porch of the Tipsy Turtle Bar. The bar's decor reflects the club mood, "barefoot British," with burgees hanging from the ceiling and dollar bills plastered along the wall, all autographed by former guests from Jimmy Carter to Christopher Reeve.

Walk past the 50-foot saltwater pool with its green striped cushion lounges. Your Abaco pine cottage has carpeting, air-conditioning, and sliding glass doors ($135 double). The beach is a short walk away. If you're arriving in your own boat, you might radio ahead to reserve one of the Seaside Villas (rates on request), which may be the only "hotel rooms" in the Bahamas that let you tie up at your own dock.

Activities include boat rentals, snorkeling, windsurfing, bonefishing, and deep-sea fishing. No tennis or golf. The two biggest weeks of the year are the June fishing tournament and the July regatta.

Green Turtle Club, Green Turtle Cay, Abaco, Bahamas. (305) 842–3109 or (809) 367–2572.

Bluff House is an elegant hideaway on Green Turtle Cay. When you arrive by boat, you have a short uphill hike through tall trees to the main building. The handsome lounge has wicker chairs with floral cushions and a louvered glass wall looking out onto the 40-foot pool. The dining room has ceramic tile floors, beamed ceilings, and a sea view.

People come to Bluff House for the seclusion and natural beauty. Rates range from $75 (standard double) to $226 (three-bedroom villa with kitchen). Suites ($106) are the most popular of the resort's 36 rooms. That means a bedroom with pickled-pine paneling, a pine staircase leading down to the living room, and a kitchenette and patio on the sea.

Tennis, boat rentals, sailing, bonefishing, deep-sea fishing, and windsurfing are among the activities to choose from. Your hosts are the owners, Melissa and Leslie Davies.

Bluff House, Green Turtle Cay, Abaco, Bahamas. (305) 941–6987.

NEW PLYMOUTH

Wherever you stay, you must visit the village of New Plymouth on Green Turtle Cay. The ferry takes you there. New Plymouth is an excellent place to meet people; the list of sights is so well established that you'll keep running into the same people all day.

There are two must-sees in town. One, right at the end of the ferry dock, is the **Albert Lowe Museum.** This small house behind the white picket fence is chock-full of Abaco history. The local artist Alton Lowe named it for his father, whose paintings of local subjects are inside. You'll also find six rooms filled with photos and artifacts designed to help preserve the island's culture.

You must not leave without visiting **Miss Emily's Blue Bee Bar.** Just turn left as you enter town, make a left at the cemetery, and you're there. Miss Emily's looks run-down compared to the pink, mustard-yellow, and pistachio-green houses nearby, but a lot of famous people have been here and left their photos and business cards to paper the walls. Have a Goombay Smash and hope to meet someone sexy from the yacht next door.

MARSH HARBOUR

The Abacos' other center of tourism is in Marsh Harbour. Fly or take a boat; getting there overland from Treasure Cay is a 20-mile trek over incredibly bumpy roads. Taxi drivers charge $70 or more round-trip, and they deserve every cent.

The **Conch Inn** has been the boaters' social center here for years. In the Conch Crawl, where you can have breakfast, drinks, or lunch, bulletin-board messages, mail for the regulars, and ship-to-shore radio calls are constantly coming in. In late afternoon, make new friends poolside by watching or joining in the daily Wallyball game (named for former owner Wally Smith, but also a play on words: Bahamians pronounce their Vs as Ws).

The Conch Inn restaurant, in a separate building, is *the* place for dinner. Its Conch Out Bar offers an attractive living-room setting, all white with hot pink and yellow accents. The restaurant itself has a combination of wicker chairs and director's chairs at white tables, and bamboo shades rolled high so diners can gaze into the harbor. Specialties include the seafood plate (conch, shrimp, and grouper) and turtle steak.

The inn's decor is nothing to write home about, but each room is air-conditioned and clean. The year-round rate is $70 double. Conch Inn Resort, Box 434, Marsh Harbour, Abaco, Bahamas. (809) 367–2800.

The **Great Abaco Beach Hotel** is a much more elegant Marsh Harbour address. At first you see only a long dirt road, then the grand green lawn appears, dotted with towering palm trees bent by the winds. The pool and white-sand beach are just beyond.

The rooms at Great Abaco ($135 double) are luxurious by Out Island standards. They're spacious, with air-conditioning, carpeting, two double beds with bamboo headboards, print draperies, and a bath with a separate dressing area. Every room has a beach-view balcony. Each villa ($165–$195) has a living room, bedroom, open kitchen, and Abaco pine deck.

On the nights the Dolphin Bar has live music, you'll find a lively, youngish crowd of tourists and locals dancing the early morning hours away. If you meet someone nice there, the next move might be a candlelight dinner the following evening in the large lobby-level dining room. Red banquettes, hanging plants, and a pine cathedral ceiling provide the setting for lobster, turtle steak, and a special Caesar salad for two.

Activities include tennis, snorkeling, diving, fishing trips, bike rentals, and sailboat charters (with or without crew).

Great Abaco Beach Hotel, Box 419, Marsh Harbour, Abaco, Bahamas. (809) 367–2158.

HOPE TOWN

A more secluded area near Marsh Harbour is Hope Town on Elbow Cay (accessible by ferry), where there are three hotels to choose from.

Hope Town Harbour Lodge looks as though it belongs in a New England seaside resort. This white clapboard house with pink trim has 19 carpeted hotel rooms ($70–$85 double) and one entire house ($650 per week). If you need air-conditioning, ask for one of the downstairs rooms (#1–5, 9, and 14).

The dining room menu changes every night. Your choices will be Continental, perhaps grouper Dijonnaise or veal piccata. The Pool Bar is the site of the hotel's locally famous Sunday champagne brunch. If you're staying here, you automatically get reservations to the huge buffet. Otherwise, write or radio a week or two ahead of time. The ferry lets you off at the hotel's front door.

Hope Town Harbour Lodge, Hope Town, Abaco, Bahamas. (809) 367–2277 or (800) 626–5690.

The **Abaco Inn** is one of those places that wouldn't impress you if you saw it vacant, but it draws the right people to its splendid isolation and overcomes the landscape. There are only 10 cottages, so reserve ahead for what you want. All the oceanfront cottages ($115 double) have king-size beds, bookshelves, walk-in open closets, baths with shower only, beamed ceilings, and ceiling fans. If you want privacy, ask for #5; it faces the ocean directly, and you can relax in your own hammock, hidden by foliage. The harbor rooms ($95) offer the same features, plus sliding glass doors and air-conditioning. The best two, #9 and #7, face the bay directly.

You might spend your days at the saltwater pool, perched dramatically on a cliff, and your evenings by the piano or fireplace in the pine-paneled lobby and lounge.

The inn offers diving, snorkeling, sailing trips, and all the usual activities, but meals are the big event. Where you eat literally depends on which way the wind is blowing; tables are set for comfort as well as view. If you aren't staying here, you can sail in for the fixed-price dinner. A recent menu offered a choice of roast duck, veal piccata, and coquille St. Jacques, plus the more unusual peanut butter soup and zucchini bread.

Your one problem could be getting there. The normal ferry takes you to Hope Town Harbour Lodge. To get to the Abaco Inn, you either ask the captain to radio ahead so the inn van will meet you there or charter a boat to take you directly to the Abaco Inn dock.

Abaco Inn, Hope Town, Elbow Cay, Abaco, Bahamas. (809) 367–2666.

The **Elbow Cay Beach Inn,** run by a charming Danish couple, has become the center of Elbow Cay's nightlife, thanks to the live music (Wednesday to Saturday nights) and the smorgasbord. Other assets include a freshwater pool and a 38-foot boat, so guests can go diving or snorkeling.

The 82-acre resort has 30 rooms ($74–$89) and, although the decor (thatched ceilings and cement bed bases in some) may not suit every taste, some of the views are spectacular. Five rooms allow you to lie in bed and look out sliding glass doors directly onto the water.

Elbow Cay Beach Inn, Hope Town, Abaco, Bahamas. (809) 367–2748.

MAN-OF-WAR CAY

The day trip not to miss is the one to Man-of-War Cay, the boat-building capital of the Bahamas. Take the same ferry that brought you to Elbow Cay (owned by the Alburys, as is most of Man-of-War) and plan to spend half a day or so. Be prepared: There are no real restaurants here, and no liquor is sold.

The roads here are no more than wide sidewalks (there are no cars), and the road to the beach is lined with shrubbery and trees.

Dock & Dine is the first building you'll see, with take-out food on one side and a dive shop on the other. The dive shop rents and sells equipment and organizes dive trips. Turn left to see examples of old-fashioned boat building. Several gift shops offer books about the area, T-shirts, and the like. The Seaside Boutique has a good selection of Androsia, some from Andros and some made here from original designs. The Sail

Shop is the one stop everyone wants to make: You can watch local women sew canvas items, then buy your favorite—bags, hats, carry-alls, or shaving kits. Finally, for great ice cream, visit the Bite Site.

For a get-away-from-it-all vacation, there are about 20 two-bedroom cottages for rent. Weekly rates usually include utilities, linens, and kitchenware. Some are on or near the beach. For information, call the Man-of-War marina, (809) 367-2306.

Getting to the Abacos: There are direct Bahamasair flights from Miami to Treasure Cay. Scheduled charters fly from Florida to Treasure Cay and Marsh Harbour. Bahamasair has daily flights from both Nassau and Miami to Marsh Harbour.

THE EXUMAS

Fly to the Exumas, if only for the view. Even scenery-weary pilots still marvel at the surrealistic blue, green, and white patterns of the Exuma cays as they are seen from the air. The shimmers, ridges, and gradations of color where islands seem to float in the air and the sea seems to blend with the sky are worth fighting for a window seat to watch (right side of the plane on your way to George Town; left side coming back).

The Exuma cays mean challenge and beauty to boaters, too; this is the yachting capital of the Bahamas. In the Exumas the bonefishing is remarkable. The snorkeling at the Exuma Land and Sea Park is breathtaking. And you can always rent a boat and find a private cay all your own.

A taxi from the George Town airport will get you to your hotel, but renting a car or a boat is a must if you're planning to see the sights.

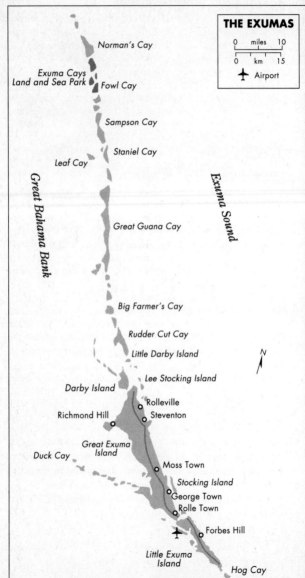

THE EXUMAS

0 miles 10

0 km 15

✈ Airport

Norman's Cay

Exuma Cays Land and Sea Park

Fowl Cay

Sampson Cay

Staniel Cay

Leaf Cay

Great Bahama Bank

Exuma Sound

Great Guana Cay

Big Farmer's Cay

Rudder Cut Cay

Little Darby Island

N

Lee Stocking Island

Darby Island

Rolleville

Richmond Hill

Steventon

Great Exuma Island

Duck Cay

Moss Town

Stocking Island

George Town

Rolle Town

✈

Forbes Hill

Little Exuma Island

Hog Cay

The first thing you'll learn is that George Town isn't a town at all but a scattering of buildings with no central district. If there is one landmark, it's the **Peace & Plenty Hotel,** a pink and white inn that began life as a sponge warehouse and was strictly a yacht club until a few decades ago.

Today it's the center of social life for yachtsmen and landlubbers alike. The cozy bar, with its blue plank banquettes, its collection of burgees, and the wooden nameplates of ships like *Fascinatin' Bitch* and *Sun Sign,* is the sort of place where everybody calls the bartenders by name. On the nights that the hotel features live music, the bar and pool deck are as raucous as a fraternity party—but with guests of all ages, races, and creeds.

Peace & Plenty's rooms are clean and pleasant and recently refurbished. A typical guest room has a tile floor, double bed, beige rattan furniture, marble vanity and shower, air-conditioning, and a good-sized balcony. Despite its modest demeanor, this was one of the first hotels in all of the Bahamas to bother with little amenities like leaving shampoo, shower cap, and scented English soap in the bath for each new guest.

There are eight waterfront rooms (#5, 6, 9, 10, 15, 16, 20, and 21) at $98 per day, double. But for $4 less per day, rooms #17, 18, and 19 give you almost as good a sea view. Three poolside rooms (#1, 2, and 3) have been turned into garden suites with sitting rooms whose sliding glass doors open onto the pool area.

The pool here is small, as are all Exuma hotel pools. What you'll want to do is take the ferry (free to hotel guests) to Stocking Island, where a stretch of white-sand beach that's perfect for sunning and swimming awaits you. Pick the right morning or the right cove, and it could be just you and a long-legged sea bird among the pines and sand dunes. The "beach club" here is a one-room wooden shelter that serves sandwiches and drinks. This is the perfect island for that romantic picnic for two.

Meals in the Peace & Plenty are as casual as the restaurant's blue and white lawn furniture decor—until evening. Then it's a formal five-course dinner that you order by writing out your own dinner check.

Peace & Plenty Hotel, Box 55, George Town, Exuma, Bahamas. (305) 462–2551 or (809) 336–2551.

George Town's few shops are right across the street. **Sandpiper** has an excellent selection of paperbacks from Hemingway to Harold Robbins, plus books about the Bahamas, resort wear, and silk screens done by the owner. The **Peace & Plenty Boutique** has a large selection of Androsia batik resort wear.

The **Pieces of 8 Hotel** is a motel-like building set on a hill so that every room has a sea view. The 33 rooms ($60, single or double) have balconies, carpet, air-conditioning, and sliding-door closets. The glass-walled restaurant, overlooking the pool, serves all three meals. A dive operation is run in the building across the street.

The **Out Island Inn** just down the road, its sister operation, is by far the more glamorous of the two. You'll enter via a curving, tree-lined driveway and probably spot the pool and tennis courts before being taken to your room.

Each of the 88 air-conditioned rooms ($220 double, Full American Plan) has two double beds, a carpet, balcony, bath with marble vanity, and a dressing table with the mirror and the plugs in the right places. Louvered floor-to-ceiling windows give the exteriors an almost Japanese look, and greenery growing on the stone walls adds an unusual ivy-covered campus touch.

The Reef Bar is the inn's huge seaside restaurant, set on its own peninsula. You'll find typically nautical decor, casual food at lunch, more ambitious dishes like beef medallions topped with crabmeat and Monterey Jack cheese at dinner, and a lot of action on the nights they have live music. The stone pier right outside provides a place to fish—or to watch the seagulls taking a break.

Back in "town," you'll find the **Two Turtles Inn.** Valerie Noyes, the charming British woman who welcomed guests from Prince Philip to King Constantine of Greece during her years at Peace & Plenty, became manager a few years ago and promptly began to transform a somewhat rundown property into a European-style inn. It was the first hotel in the Exumas to offer satellite TV.

The 14 rooms ($68 double) all have one double bed and one twin, plus carpeting, a bath with shower, and ceiling fans. Only rooms #10, 11, 12, 14, and 15 are air-conditioned. Reserve ahead to get one of the four efficiencies (same price) with kitchenettes behind louvered doors.

Meals (burgers to lobster) are served inside the half-timbered dining room or in the shady central courtyard.

Two Turtles Inn, Box 51, George Town, Exuma, Bahamas. (809) 336-2545.

The **Regatta Point Apartments,** just past the government dock road, is a lovely place to stay, particularly if you're planning to do your own cooking. A palm-lined driveway leads to the five-room building. The two rooms downstairs are large efficiencies (about 23' by 15') with open kitchen, louvered closets, and bathrooms with back doors (the better to track water and sand into, rather than into the main room). Each suite has high ceilings, tile floors, a full kitchen behind louvered doors, a separate bedroom, a bath with a large vanity, and a back door to the patio. All rooms are $76 double; the early birds get the suites.

Despite the name and location, this is not where the revelers stay at Regatta time. Expect a quieter, almost pastoral mood with a tiny beach and a spectacular sea view.

Regatta Point Apartments, Box 6, George Town, Exuma, Bahamas. (809) 336-2206.

The place for authentic Bahamian food is **Eddie's Edgewater Club.** Turn left at "the pond" (Victoria Lake) and keep going until you see a green building, usually with lots of local men hanging around outside. This is a family place (Victor and Andrea Brown run it; the original Eddie is Andrea's father), but it can look rough, and women probably won't feel comfortable alone here. Popular dishes include lobster, chicken livers, turtle steak, and red snapper. The very Bahamian weekend special is chicken, sheep tongue, or turtle souse. No credit cards.

The new hotel in the Exumas is the **Flamingo Bay Hotel and Villas,** located near the airport and just outside George Town. The mansionlike main building has only three rooms ($85–$125 night) and two suites ($125–$200 night), the suites accommodating as many as four people.

Fourteen villas are available for rental, but they tend to be taken on long-term leases, so you will need to call well in advance for availability and prices. The four one-bedroom villas start at about $100 a day; the single four-bedroom villa ranges from $500 to $600 a day. The nine other villas all have two bedrooms.

All Flamingo Bay accommodations have air-conditioning, satellite TV, and direct dialing to the USA. The resort has one tennis court, private beaches, and boats for rent.

Flamingo Bay Hotel and Villas, Box 90, George Town, Exuma, Bahamas. (809) 336–2661 or (800) 338–8588. Flamingo Bay, 260 Crandon Blvd., Unit 24, Key Biscayne, FL 33149. (305) 361–8588.

It may be only a matter of time until the Exumas are discovered by vacationers other than the loyal yachting set. George Town is on Great Exuma, which is only one island in a 150-mile-long chain of more than 300 islands. Many of the islands are small and uninhabited. Fortunately for those who hold the Exumas close to their hearts, this destination has a long way to go before it risks losing its rustic Out Island charm.

When you feel like sightseeing, drive to the north of Great Exuma toward Rolleville, preferably with a guide who can identify the old plantations and other historical sights along the way. **Fisherman's Inn** is the popular place to lunch on this part of the island.

There are scheduled charter flights to George Town from Fort Lauderdale, Miami, and Eleuthera (North Eleuthera and Rock Sound). Bahamasair flies here from Nassau.

ANDROS

You won't have to tell the taxi driver where you're going. If you are American or European and getting off a plane in Andros Town, he'll approach and ask, **"Small Hope Bay Lodge?"** and he'll be right. Although Andros is the largest of the Bahamian islands, it is one of the least explored. Small Hope is one of its few real resorts.

Most of the guests at Small Hope are avid or avidly aspiring scuba divers. The world's third largest barrier reef is here, and the underwater beauty is dazzling enough at 10 or 15 feet to convince novices to don tank and regulator for a shallow dive.

Others swear they'd come here for the dinner conversation alone. The North American owners Dick and Rosi Birch are gradually passing the torch to a new generation—his kids, hers, and theirs, now grown, ably running the show, and continuing to set a special tone.

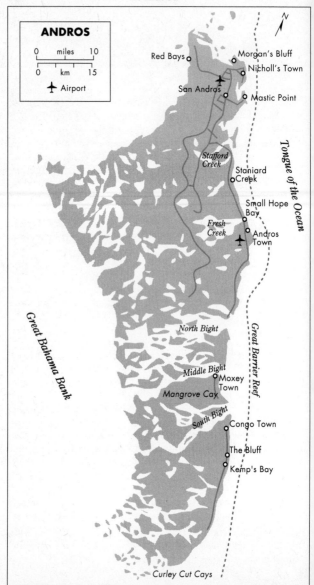

ANDROS

| 0 | miles | 10 |
| 0 | km | 15 |

✈ Airport

Red Bays ○

Morgan's Bluff ○
Nicholl's Town ○

✈

San Andros ○

Mastic Point ○

Stafford Creek

Staniard ○ Creek

Small Hope Bay ○

Fresh Creek ○

✈ Andros Town

Tongue of the Ocean

North Bight

Middle Bight ○
Moxey Town

Mangrove Cay

South Bight ○ Congo Town

The Bluff ○
Kemp's Bay ○

Great Bahama Bank

Great Barrier Reef

Curley Cut Cays

If you've never been to one of these 20-cottage resorts with honor bars and first-name informality, consider what may well be your typical day:

You wake up early, an ocean breeze rustling through your Androsia batik curtains. You could compare your cottage to a hotel room and find it a bit too rustic, but you've already mellowed (this happens within 24 hours here). So you see it instead as the camp cabin of your childhood, redecorated for adult life with carpeting, thick towels, Androsia pillowcases, and wall hangings. Some cabins even have water beds.

You dress in a swimsuit and cover-up or T-shirt, then stroll to the main building for breakfast. The dining and gathering room has a beamed ceiling, louvered windows on all sides, and a stone fireplace. There are six tables, most for six people each, and pine-plank chairs. Help yourself to juice, coffee, cereal, and toast, then order eggs or waffles from the kitchen.

The morning dive boat leaves from the pier at 9:30, heading for a deep dive and a shallow one. If you're not a diver, you will have the resort to yourself. The others will be back just in time for lunch.

When it's time for a prelunch drink, you pour yourself a beer or glass of wine or mix yourself a drink at the bar, take the card that has your name on it out of the slot, write in what you've had, and carry your glass to a lawn chair in the shade.

Lunch is indoors, buffet-style. As soon as you've finished, it's time to think about the afternoon dive. Or you might skip the dive that day to lie on the beach, wind down in the hot tub, or schedule a Swedish massage.

The others will be back in time to "dress" for dinner. When you wash out your wet swimsuits and T-shirts, there are pegs outside your door to hang them on for fresh-air drying. On a dark night, this can help you to identify your cabin on the way home.

Conch fritters are served at cocktail hour. Be sure to get there early; they go fast. Dinner is usually a choice of meat or seafood entree, preceded by a buffet of appetizers. Afterward, guests chat, deal the cards, or get out a board game.

Feel like a nightcap? Pour yourself a Courvoisier, sign for it, and stroll home in the moonlight. This can't be camp.

When did the counselor ever let you bring brandy back to the room or offer nightly turndown service?

The resort also offers all-day trips that go out at 9:30 A.M. and return around 4:30 P.M. Each trip includes a morning dive, an afternoon dive, and a packed lunch served on an island where guests can swim, lie on the beach, or snorkel.

Warning: Don't bring fancy clothes to Small Hope Bay. Dressing for dinner generally means taking a shower. Rosi Birch herself is likely to turn up barefoot in one of her long Androsia batik dresses (she is the founder and owner of Androsia). High-heel sandals for women seem formal here. Remember, your cabin's front lawn is the beach, and you'll just get sand in your shoes if you wear them.

The beach and the swimming from shore aren't much, but swimming from the dive boat in clear, cool water on perfect sky-blue days makes up for it. The daytime landscape is far from lush, but the night sky is so clear that many visitors spot stars they've never seen before. A frog might turn up in your bathroom, but he'll leave peacefully.

Small Hope is "a world of its own," yet guests are secluded from the outside world, not from each other. And when someone feels a need for more action, they head for the local disco.

Summer isn't off-season for the divers who come here. You won't find many singles (check the names and room numbers on the honor-bar slots to see who's alone), but you're unlikely to be lonely if you come alone. The couples and families from all across the USA are a relatively sophisticated and friendly bunch.

Summer rates ($224 double) include three meals, round-trip transfers, and the use of sailboat, windsurfing equipment, and hot tub. Dives are extra, but the resort offers packages that include them. One such midwinter seven-day package last season was $1,000.

You can fly here from Nassau by Bahamasair. There are also charters, including Small Hope's own plane, directly from Fort Lauderdale.

Small Hope Bay Lodge, Box N-1131, Nassau, Bahamas, or Box 21667, Fort Lauderdale, FL 33335. (800) 223–6961, (305) 463–9130, or (809) 368–2014.

If you have a chance to explore the dense forests of Andros, keep your eyes open for Chickcharnies. They're the legendary red-eyed elves who hang by their tails from trees, can turn their heads 360 degrees on their shoulders, and create all kinds of mischief.

BIMINI

Bimini breaks all the rules for what a Bahamian island is supposed to be. In a way, little has changed here since Ernest Hemingway spent much of the 1930s on or near Bimini's waters—waters that inspired him to write *The Old Man and the Sea* and to set his *Islands in the Stream* novella here. Bimini is still the big-game fishing capital of the world; the average visitor is a Florida fisherman who stays just 1.7 days.

Bimini's location, just 50 miles off the Florida coast, earns it the nickname, "Gateway to the Bahamas." And it is certainly the most Americanized of the islands.

Current American rock hits blare from storefronts along North Bimini's main street. The barmaid at the Red Lion Pub stands under a Miami Dolphins poster as she watches the afternoon soaps. One hotelier claims he's never seen a single dollar of Bahamian currency cross his front desk.

BIMINI

0 — miles — 1
0 — km — 2
✈ Airport

East Wells

North Bimini

Paradise Point

The Sound

Straits of Florida

Porgy Bay

Bonefish Hole

Bailey Town

Pigeon Cay

Alice Town

N

South Bimini

Cavelle Pond

Nixon's Harbour

Round Rock

Summer is high season in Bimini. The time to go for blue or white marlin is April through July; for broadbill swordfish, June through September; and for snapper, April through September. Nevertheless this is a year-round destination. Bonefishing is good throughout the year, and wahoo, grouper, snapper, barracuda, dolphin, and shark are at their most catchable in the winter.

The **Bimini Big Game Fishing Club** is the place to stay. This haven of taste in what the brochures refer to as a "downto-earth salty" ("rowdy" might be more accurate) town maintains a members-only atmosphere behind its black gates.

Whether you plan to spend your days battling with marlin or basking in the sun, you'll appreciate the hotel's 23-footlong balconied rooms with carpet, air-conditioning, and modern furniture. All have two beds and are decorated with a "studio" feel—because so much entertaining (read: partying) goes on in the rooms themselves.

The club's cottages are nicer, with kitchenettes (sink and fridge only) and louver-door closets. The resort's three suites, the most glamorous lodgings of all, each have a modern living room, kitchenette, bedroom with terrace, bath, and separate dressing room. All rooms have cable TV.

Most guests are out in their boats at midday, and BBGFC will prepare box lunches for them. For those who stay behind to enjoy the tennis court or the pool with its brick deck, light lunches are available—sandwiches, salads, and a choice of hot dishes.

Dinner is the main event. Entrees in the pool-view dining room range from cracked conch to grilled lobster tails. Baby Coho salmon is flown in from Washington state.

You don't have to be wealthy to stay here, but many guests are. Chartering the resort's 41-foot *Sir Tones II* can cost more than $600 per day. At least one package vacation here, however, includes a complimentary day's rental of a 16-foot center console outboard boat.

Rooms are $98, cottages $118, and penthouses $225, double or single. Marina dockage is 60 cents per foot per day; small craft up to 30 feet long are $18 per day. 2857 S.W. 27th Ave., Miami, FL 33133. (800) 327–4149, (809) 347–2391, or (305) 444–7480.

Most guests arrive in their own boats or by ferry. Some come by seaplane.

Let's get our geography straight: "The Biminis" are two islands, north and south. Besides the airport, the only thing to see in South Bimini is a pond believed to be the Fountain of Youth that Ponce De Leon tried to find. North Bimini is the place you'll visit, and Alice Town is its one-street "capital."

Flying here from Miami, Fort Lauderdale, or Paradise Island via Chalk's seaplane can be an interesting experience. The aircraft interior is cramped, but takeoffs and landings—with sea spray covering your window—are exciting. Unless your luggage is heavy, you can walk anywhere you want to go from here. The local taxi is a van that charges $3, no matter how long or short your trip.

The first important spot you'll encounter is the **Hi*Star Disco** on your right. This stone building looks quiet enough by day, but at night it's the center of action until 3 A.M.

Bimini is not made for shopping sprees. Among the several small stores that line the street is a branch of the **Perfume Bar.**

The Compleat Angler, a dark green and white house on the left, is your first glimpse of the Bimini that Hemingway knew. Sadly, the hotel once saw fit to paint the words, "Home of Papa Ernest Hemingway" in huge letters on the building front.

Still, a place where the office and the bar are the same room can't be all bad. This bar is air-conditioned, its dark wood walls covered with an odd assortment of objects that range from straw hats to a fake shark's head. The wood is from kegs used during Bimini's rum-running heyday. This is the sort of place you'll feel effete ordering a glass of white wine.

The front room, with its fireplace and backgammon boards, holds photos of Hemingway and friends landing the big ones almost half a century ago. The Ponce de Leon bar in *Islands in the Stream* was patterned after this very place.

The Compleat Angler still qualifies as charming. The 15 air-conditioned guest rooms won't win prizes for luxury, but the price is right: $55 single, $65–$70 double. You can even rent Hemingway's old room (#1).

Compleat Angler Hotel, Box 601, Alice Town, Bimini, Bahamas. (809) 347–2122.

The Anchorage is an attractive hillside house a little further on, all fresh white paint and blue trim, an excellent lunch or dinner spot. The dining room has a spectacular view of blue-green sea; entrees range from omelets to steak or lobster. You can order a box lunch, and the marina can charter you a 28-foot boat with captain and mate.

Bimini's Blue Water Ltd., Box 627, Bimini, Bahamas. (809) 347–2166.

The **Red Lion Pub** is on your right, just a bit up the road. This is an authentically down-home place with faded wallpaper and old red diner booths. The air-conditioned bayfront dining room is a good spot for a casual lunch or dinner (served from 6 P.M. on, Tuesdays through Sundays). Entrees range from chopped sirloin to lobster tails, steak, or shrimp.

Bimini is one of the most casual of the Bahamian islands. Men shouldn't bother bringing jackets, much less ties. A dress code for dinner usually means that shoes are absolutely mandatory.

For the non-fisherperson, there is excellent scuba diving here. The most famous sight is a submerged stone wall off North Bimini, believed by some to be part of the lost continent of Atlantis.

MORE FAMILY

ISLANDS

Everyone who writes about the Bahamas likes to mention that there are 700 islands. Some of them are barely large enough to pitch a tent on, yet a number of the others have special sights, sounds, and experiences to offer. Even more undiscovered than the islands we've reported on so far, they range from a naturalist's preserve to the spot where Columbus discovered the New World (although the precise location of that event has been called into question). When you're truly ready to leave civilization behind for a week or two, one of these smaller islands could be the unspoiled vacation paradise you've been hoping to find.

ACKLINS ISLAND AND CROOKED ISLAND

Dotted with old lighthouses and separated only by a narrow passage (which you can cross by ferry), Acklins Island and Crooked Island in the southern Bahamas can be considered one destination. Completely away from the Bahamas tourist circuit, this may well be the most peaceful vacation spot you could find.

The largest resort (16 rooms) is **Pittstown Point Landings Inn** at Crooked Island's northern tip. There you'll find diving, snorkeling, and boating. Double rooms are $75–$85.

Pittstown Point Landings Inn, c/o Bahamas Caribbean International, Box 9831, Mobile, AL 36691. (205) 666–4482 or (800) 336–2507.

There are two Bahamasair flights per week between Nassau and the Colonel Hill Airport on Crooked Island, as well as weekly mailboat service.

THE BERRY ISLANDS

Lying between Bimini and Nassau, the Berry Islands get their share of visitors—primarily divers, boaters, and fishermen who know by word of mouth what the area has to offer. The 12-square-mile island's one resort, a superb one, is the **Chub Cay Club,** located on the chain's southernmost cay. The club boasts 55 rooms and villas, a complete scuba diving program, two tennis courts, and a 75-slip marina. Double rooms are $75.

Chub Cay Club, Box 661067, Miami Springs, FL 33166. (809) 32–51490 or (305) 445–7830.

The resort offers charter flights from Miami and Fort Lauderdale.

CAT ISLAND

At 200 feet above sea level, Cat Island doesn't look like the Bahamas. It has towering cliffs, thick forests, the ruins of colonial plantations, and a couple of pleasant—but very small—resorts.

Fernandez Bay Village is a 17-room property of one-bedroom cottages and two- and three-bedroom villas. Located on the bay's white-sand beach, it has a beach bar, a restaurant, and a general store. Prices start at $120 double.

Fernandez Bay Village, Box 2126, Fort Lauderdale, FL 33303. (305) 764–6945.

Greenwood Inn at Port Howe ($100 Modified American Plan) has 16 rooms. You'll find boating, snorkeling, fishing, bicycling, a pool, the beach, and even a disco here. You're six miles from Cutlass Bay, the island's southernmost settlement.

Greenwood Inn, Port Howe, Cat Island, Bahamas; write or cable for reservations.

There are two Bahamasair flights per week between Nassau and Arthur's Town (at Cat Island's northern tip). Two mail boats offer weekly service.

GREAT INAGUA

The most southerly of the Bahama islands, Great Inagua comes very close to being a naturalist's heaven. Here, at Lake Windsor, you'll find the largest colony (20,000-plus) of West Indian flamingoes in the world. Great Inagua's 234-square-mile wildlife reserve, which you can circuit by jeep tours, has rare parrots, tree ducks, pelicans, blue heron, boar, and roseate spoonbills.

There are two guest houses, with a total of 13 rooms, in Matthew Town. **Ford's Inagua Inn** (telephone 277), just a mile from the airport, has five rooms, its own marina, and a nearby beach. Double rooms are $35. **Main House** (telephone 267), half a mile away, has eight rooms, air-conditioning, and a dining room. Double rooms are $40. The address for either is simply Matthew Town, Great Inagua, Bahamas.

The only trouble is, you can't take a day trip here unless you have your own boat or plane. Bahamasair has two flights per week between Nassau and Matthew Town; if you come on Saturday, you have to stay until Tuesday.

LONG ISLAND

Long Island lies just south of Exuma, attracting many of that island's yachtsmen to its varied landscape. Divers and fishermen come, too, to enjoy their sports and to sightsee among the churches, caves, and old plantations. Nature-lovers will want to visit Conception Island, just off Stella Maris, a sanctuary for birds and green turtles.

The 60-room **Stella Maris Inn** ($76 double) is the resort of note, with fishing, boating, diving, snorkeling, waterskiing, tennis, a pool, and its own beach.

Stella Maris Inn, Stella Maris 30–105, Long Island, Bahamas. (809) 336–2106 or (809) 223–6510.

There are four Bahamasair flights per week between Nassau, Stella Maris, and Deadman's Cay (the airport farther south on Long Island). Mail-boat service runs between Nassau and Long Island at least once every two weeks.

RUM CAY

Just off Long Island's northeastern coast, Rum Cay (only 12 miles by seven) has a thriving dive resort. The 19-room **Rum Cay Club** ($109 double) specializes in scuba diving packages and offers catamarans, Windsurfers, fishing, snorkeling, and lots of deserted beach. A hot tub, a game room, and—for serious underwater photographers—a photo lab are all available.

Rum Cay Club, Box 22396, Fort Lauderdale, FL 33315. (305) 467–8355 or (800) 334–6869.

Some guests fly Bahamasair to Long Island or San Salvador, then take private planes from there. Those who buy package vacations take charter flights from Fort Lauderdale straight to Rum Cay.

SAN SALVADOR

The island of San Salvador is just as small as Rum Cay and virtually untouched, but you can hardly call it undiscovered. It was here that Christopher Columbus set foot on October 12, 1492. However, new evidence presented a few years ago challenges this longtime belief and puts the spot on another Bahamian cay 65 miles away. Yet tradition dies hard, and you can still visit the Cross Monument, where Columbus *may* have come ashore.

Whatever the truth may be, world-traveler fishermen, divers, and boaters consider San Salvador a real find. Its one resort, the highly respected **Riding Rock Inn,** (24 rooms) reopened under new management two seasons ago. Double rooms are $120 per person, Modified American Plan. Riding Rock Inn, San Salvador, Bahamas. (809) 332–2631.

Bahamasair has two flights per week between Nassau and San Salvador; there is also weekly mail-boat service from Nassau.

Index

Fodor's Travel Guides

U.S. Guides

Alaska
American Cities
The American South
Arizona
Atlantic City & the
  New Jersey Shore
Boston
California
Cape Cod
Carolinas & the
  Georgia Coast
Chesapeake
Chicago
Colorado
Dallas & Fort Worth
Disney World & the
  Orlando Area

The Far West
Florida
Greater Miami,
  Fort Lauderdale,
  Palm Beach
Hawaii
Hawaii *(Great Travel
  Values)*
Houston & Galveston
I-10: California to
  Florida
I-55: Chicago to New
  Orleans
I-75: Michigan to
  Florida
I-80: San Francisco to
  New York

I-95: Maine to Miami
Las Vegas
Los Angeles, Orange
  County, Palm Springs
Maui
New England
New Mexico
New Orleans
New Orleans *(Pocket
  Guide)*
New York City
New York City *(Pocket
  Guide)*
New York State
Pacific North Coast
Philadelphia
Puerto Rico *(Fun in)*

Rockies
San Diego
San Francisco
San Francisco *(Pocket
  Guide)*
Texas
United States of
  America
Virgin Islands
  (U.S. & British)
Virginia
Waikiki
Washington, DC
Williamsburg,
  Jamestown &
  Yorktown

Foreign Guides

Acapulco
Amsterdam
Australia, New Zealand
  & the South Pacific
Austria
The Bahamas
The Bahamas *(Pocket
  Guide)*
Barbados *(Fun in)*
Beijing, Guangzhou &
  Shanghai
Belgium & Luxembourg
Bermuda
Brazil
Britain *(Great Travel
  Values)*
Canada
Canada *(Great Travel
  Values)*
Canada's Maritime
  Provinces
Cancún, Cozumel,
  Mérida, The
  Yucatán
Caribbean
Caribbean *(Great
  Travel Values)*

Central America
Copenhagen,
  Stockholm, Oslo,
  Helsinki, Reykjavik
Eastern Europe
Egypt
Europe
Europe *(Budget)*
Florence & Venice
France
France *(Great Travel
  Values)*
Germany
Germany *(Great Travel
  Values)*
Great Britain
Greece
Holland
Hong Kong & Macau
Hungary
India
Ireland
Israel
Italy
Italy *(Great Travel
  Values)*
Jamaica *(Fun in)*

Japan
Japan *(Great Travel
  Values)*
Jordan & the Holy Land
Kenya
Korea
Lisbon
Loire Valley
London
London *(Pocket Guide)*
London *(Great Travel
  Values)*
Madrid
Mexico
Mexico *(Great Travel
  Values)*
Mexico City & Acapulco
Mexico's Baja & Puerto
  Vallarta, Mazatlán,
  Manzanillo, Copper
  Canyon
Montreal
Munich
New Zealand
North Africa
Paris
Paris *(Pocket Guide)*

People's Republic of
  China
Portugal
Province of Quebec
Rio de Janeiro
The Riviera *(Fun on)*
Rome
St. Martin/St. Maarte
Scandinavia
Scotland
Singapore
South America
South Pacific
Southeast Asia
Soviet Union
Spain
Spain *(Great Travel
  Values)*
Sweden
Switzerland
Sydney
Tokyo
Toronto
Turkey
Vienna
Yugoslavia

Special-Interest Guides

Bed & Breakfast
Guide: North America
1936…On the
  Continent

Royalty Watching
Selected Hotels of
Europe

Selected Resorts
  and Hotels of the U.S.
Ski Resorts of North
  America

Views to Dine by
  around the World